christmas in ireland

christmas in ireland

from world book

World Book Encyclopedia, Inc.
a Scott Fetzer company
Chicago

staff

Publisher
William H. Nault

Editorial
Editor in chief
Robert O. Zeleny

Managing editor
Harry R. Snowden Jr.

Senior editor
Scott Thomas

Rights and permissions
Janet T. Peterson

Editorial assistant
Valerie Adams

Writer
Rena Moran

Product production
Executive director
Peter Mollman

Manufacturing
Joseph C. LaCount

Research and development
Henry Koval

Pre-press services
Jerry Stack

Production control
Janice M. Rossing

Film separation
Alfred J. Mozdzen

Art
Executive director
William Hammond

Art director
Roberta Dimmer

Assistant art director
Joe Gound

Designer
Alexandra Kalantzis

Photography director
John S. Marshall

Photographs editor
Sandra Ozanick

The editors wish to thank the many people who took part in the development of this book. Special appreciation goes to Peggy Boyle, James C. Burke, Bob Burns, Father Martin Dwan, Michael Gaffey, Ken Horan, Father Cathal McBride, Kathy McDonnell, Kathleen O'Callaghan, Jim O'Neill, Patrick Roche, Kathleen Rolfe, Kay Ann Woulfe, Michael Woulfe, and Martin Woulfe.

contents

the colors
of christmas

The Irish consider Christmas the most holy and joyous time of the year. The season is, in fact, so joyous that Epiphany, the last of the twelve days of Christmas, is viewed with melancholy simply because it is the end. Christmas in Ireland is a joyful time, and yet many of the traditions and customs associated with the holiday are touched with that same spirit of melancholy that colors Epiphany.

The Irish have a saying: "A green Christmas makes a fat churchyard." A Christmas without snow is an augury, a sign, of hard times to come, an omen that the village churchyards will grow fat with new graves. The proverb reveals something of the character of the Irish people, and it reveals something of their history and struggles. It does not snow often in Ireland, and thus, it does not snow often on Christmas. A green Christmas is the norm, rather than the exception. Through much of the history of Ireland, fat churchyards were the norm, rather than the exception. And this struggle for survival, constant through hundreds of years, is reflected in the Irish celebration of even this most happy of holidays.

The Irish, of course, have another saying about snow on Christmas: "When it snows on Christmas Eve, the angels in heaven are plucking geese for the feast on the morrow." A white Christmas makes a thin churchyard. When it snows on Christmas, there will be a goose for dinner; there will be plenty through the coming year. Both proverbs say the same thing, but one speaks of a cup half empty; the other of a cup half full. The ability to look at something in two ways, one bitter and the other sweet, also reveals something of the character of the Irish. Christmas, like life, can be white and joyous; it can be green and melancholy; or, more likely, it can, and will, be both.

On Christmas Eve, the Irish put lighted candles in their windows. There is, of course, a reason. In Ireland, there is always a reason, always a story behind the custom. The candles, it is said, light the way for Mary and Joseph, who wander forever on Christmas Eve. But in the days when the English tried to suppress Roman Catholicism, the candles were a signal to passing priests of a house where Mass could be said in safety. So, to the Irish, the candles symbolize two things at once. One is joyous. One is sad.

On Christmas night, there is another custom—the telling of stories. The oldest member of the family gathers everyone around the hearth or the table and recounts the story of Mary and Joseph. The tales, of course, don't stop at Bethlehem. There are yarns about the family, about the famine, about the great heroes and villains of Irish history, and even about the rocks and bogs and hills of the countryside. The possibilities are endless, because Irish folklore is endless. While the Swedes have 25 versions of the Cinderella story, the Irish have 311 and are still counting. Christmas night is not, of course, the only appropriate time for storytelling. Any occasion will do, and the Irish have a story for any and every occasion, for every event of life.

There is, naturally, a story behind all of this storytelling. For centuries, Irish children were deprived of an education either by poverty or by English law. The English believed that the Irish might be less troublesome if they were kept illiterate. The Irish, perhaps rebellious by nature, combated this business by conducting classes in secret in the countryside. Hidden behind bushes and hedges, priests taught a few children of every generation to read and write.

The Irish people's second, and most significant, defense against their lack of education was storytelling. By making up a story for every occasion, by extracting the meaning from every event of life and turning that understanding into a parable, the Irish preserved their culture and taught their children a sense of history, justice, and identity. Every village, no matter how small, had a professional storyteller, the shanachie (SHAN uh kee), who memorized the entire repertoire of village tales. He then passed the tales on to the children and on to the next shanachie. If life was short and bitter, the memory of that life was not. Filled with victory and joy, the memory became a living thread that passed through the consciousness of generations of Irish men and women. As long as the stories survived, the lives and events that inspired them survived and had meaning.

This system for preserving history and the collective wisdom of life is by no means unique. All tribes and cultures produce folklore. But in Ireland, the results were extraordinary. Storytellers beget storytellers. And the Irish begot a line of storytellers that rivals that of any country on earth: Jonathan Swift, Oliver Goldsmith, Richard Brinsley Sheridan, Oscar Wilde, George Moore, William Butler Yeats, George Bernard Shaw, Liam O'Flaherty, Frank O'Connor, James Joyce, Sean O'Casey, Brendan Behan, Samuel Beckett. And every Irish author, from Swift to Wilde to Joyce, filled his writings with that dual view, that joy interwoven with melancholy, that is characteristic of the Irish and their celebration of Christmas. Irish literature, like Irish life, is filled with laughter—but it is the kind that cuts with irony. There is always a story behind the story.

The final chapter of *Christmas in Ireland,* "The Wee Christmas Cabin of Carn-na-ween," is one of those stories that may have been retold around the hearth on Christmas night. Like most Irish tales, it is both bitter and sweet, green and white, filled with both fat churchyards and geese plucked in heaven.

A cross (left), *carved in the Celtic style, marks an ancient grave at the tenth-century monastery of St. Columba in Durrow. The Celtic style, in Ireland, is a combination of Christian symbolism and pagan patterns of interwoven curves and spirals. Christmas in Ireland is usually green, even in County Donegal* (below), *a peninsula in the northwest corner of the island.*

bringing home the christmas

The people of Ireland, officially the Republic of Ireland, are over-whelmingly Roman Catholic in religion. The word *catholic* means "universal," and the Church in Ireland is not appreciably different from the Church in Italy or in Spain. But in Ireland, the Roman Catholic Church has come to represent something beyond religion to the people. Through hundreds of years of English, Protestant rule, the people of Ireland tenaciously held to the faith that Saint Patrick introduced to the island in the A.D. 400's. The refusal of the Irish people to bend to the will of their English overlords on this one issue—their religion—became a symbol of their general resistance to domination. To the Irish, the Church became a symbol of their will for both religious and political freedom, and Christmas, the most religious of holidays, became a celebration of the two highly interwoven ideas. Although the people of the Republic of Ireland gained their freedom in 1921, the significance of Christmas in Ireland has remained unique. The season is thus doubly joyous as a celebration of the birth of the Christ child and the force of the people's will for freedom. Preparing for a holiday fraught with so much significance is no easy matter. There are traditions to be kept and standards to be maintained.

The holiday season begins, spiritually, with Advent, which includes the first four Sundays before Christmas. *Advent* comes from the Latin *adventus*, which means "a coming." It is the season when Christians remember the coming of Christ and prepare to celebrate the festival of His birth.

In Ireland, the Catholic Mass is celebrated during Advent in much the same way the Mass is celebrated during the rest of the year. However, readings and sermons during the season are related to the coming of Christ. The need to prepare spiritually for the Christmas season is also emphasized.

Advent traditionally has been a penitential season in the Roman Catholic Church; it is, like Lent, a time to confess one's sins and express sorrow for wrongdoing. Thus, the sacrament of confession takes on an added importance

11

during Advent as the faithful prepare their souls for the coming of Christ.

In Ireland, Advent was once a season for fasting. Pious Catholics limited themselves to a single meal on Wednesdays and Fridays, as well as on Christmas Eve. Some Irish Catholics still fast during Advent as a private expression of devotion. For the faithful, Advent may also be a time for extra prayers, both morning and night. In times past, children were often encouraged to say extra *Paters* and *Aves* and to keep track of the number.

Most Catholic churches in Ireland are decorated quite simply for the Christmas season. Berried holly leaves are stitched together, and these garlands are wound around pillars in the church and festooned around the edge of the altar. Children who attend the parish school may help to make the decorations for the church. Every Catholic church has a Nativity scene, also called the crib or the Bethlehem scene. The placement of the Nativity scene varies from

Irish schoolchildren (below) *participate in a holiday pantomime play, one of many theatrical performances offered in Dublin during the Christmas season. The boys' choir of St. Anne's Church, Dublin* (opposite page), *sings carols from the church's front steps during the Advent season.*

church to church, although it is usually placed near the altar or in the back of the church. Families often approach the Nativity scene as a group before being seated for Mass. Parents take this opportunity to give their children a little homily on the Nativity—an explanation of the religious and historical significance of the Bethlehem scene. People often pray or meditate while kneeling in front of the crib. In the past, worshipers would sometimes take a wisp of straw from the Nativity scene, believing that it would bring a blessing or good luck.

Christmas in Ireland requires material as well as spiritual preparation. Years ago, such preparations began many weeks before Christmas. The entire house was cleaned from top to bottom; the housewife spent days cleaning, scrubbing, sweeping, washing, scouring, and shining. The man of the house also took an active part in the Christmas preparations. First, he tidied the farmyard; next, he cleaned and usually whitewashed the outbuildings; and, finally, he attacked the farmhouse itself, whitewashing both inside and out in preparation for the coming of the Christ child. Today, most Irish families give their homes and grounds a thorough cleaning and tidying before Christmas, but few approach the job with the same zeal, the near religious devotion, as did past generations.

Christmas dinner is, traditionally, the most elaborate meal of the year in Ireland, and today, as in the past, many women begin their preparations weeks in advance. Plum puddings, with plenty of raisins, currants, spices, and bread-

At Mansion House, the residence of the Lord Mayor of Dublin, a pair of angels, members of the Little Carol Singers, announce the arrival of the Infant Jesus.

crumbs, as well as a liberal portion of Irish whiskey, are as necessary a part of the Irish Christmas feast as turkey with cranberry sauce is to the American Christmas dinner. Bread pudding, often served with butterscotch sauce, is another favorite. Cookies and tarts, crowned with a snowy skiff of confectioners' sugar, are other popular holiday treats.

The real star of the culinary season is the fantastic Christmas cake, which may be started as early as October to allow time for proper mellowing. No expense or effort is spared in making this "cake of the year." The base is caramel, to which is added dried and candied fruits, blanched almonds, citrus rind, orange-flower water, rose water, brandy, the whites of eight eggs, as well as the more mundane ingredients—flour, sugar, and butter. After the basic cake is baked and wrapped in cheesecloth or muslin, it is stored in a cool, dry place. Even this storage of the Christmas cake may involve a tradition all its own; the walls of old houses or cottages often have special bricks or stones that can be removed to provide a cubbyhole for the mellowing of the special Christmas cake. Each week before Christmas, it is removed from the wall, pierced with a knitting needle, and refortified with brandy. Two weeks before Christmas, it is

enveloped in a coating of marzipan, or almond paste. And two days before Christmas, before the actual feast, it is blanketed with icing, which the Irish call royal frosting: a blend of sugar, egg whites, acetic acid, and exactly three drops of laundry bluing—to ensure that the mixture is "as pure and white as the driven snow." This elaborate confection, besides being Christmas fare, is the traditional Irish wedding cake.

Closer to Christmas, the lady of the house shops for the traditional Christmas goose or turkey, which may be purchased, throughout most of Ireland, either freshly dressed or live. An ample supply of vegetables—potatoes, carrots, turnips, peas, and onions—are stocked for holiday cooking. The man of the house may also lay in a store of spirits—sherry, whiskey, and stout, a heavy, strong, dark-brown beer—for friends or relatives paying calls during the holidays. It is interesting to note that Christmas is the only time of the year when most Irish families keep liquor in the house. Except for the Christmas season, one would seldom be offered anything stronger than a cup of tea in an Irish home. In Ireland, drinking alone is considered unsociable, and almost all liquor is consumed in the company of friends or neighbors down at the corner or village pub.

Nearly 40 per cent of the Irish people continue to live in rural areas. For those living on farms, preparations for the Christmas feast may involve fattening the Christmas goose or turkey, rather than buying it at a market. In addition, homegrown vegetables and the farm's own dairy products may be used in preparing the Christmas dinner. In times past, farmers spent weeks gathering and preparing products to take to the Christmas market. Also called the "fair day," the Christmas market was held several days before Christmas, often on a

In Ireland, the Saturday before Christmas is, by custom, the day to "bring home the Christmas." Open-air markets offer everything—from fresh flowers (below) *to live turkeys* (opposite page)—*needed for a "good and proper" Christmas.*

Saturday. The market was important to countrypeople and town folk alike. It was the day when families gathered to "bring home the Christmas." The countrypeople brought farm products to sell—turkeys, geese, butter, eggs, and vegetables. The money they received for these goods was used to buy the sugar, spice, tea, meat, and liquor needed for the Christmas celebration. In addition, the countryfolk might purchase modest Christmas gifts: clothing, household goods, or simple toys.

Townspeople went to the market for fresh fowl, butter, eggs, and other farm products needed to prepare a proper Christmas dinner. The Christmas market also provided an opportunity to socialize and to exchange gifts with country friends and relatives. Spirits were high throughout the day, and the air was filled with the sounds of friendly greetings and wishes for the season's best.

The Christmas market also provided an occasion for shopkeepers and merchants to give gifts to their regular customers. This was done to show appreciation for the customers' patronage throughout the year. Such gifts often consisted of a selection of items that the customer had purchased regularly during the past year. For example, a grocer might give a patron a box containing flour, tea, and spices. Some shopkeepers might offer their customers a box of candles or Christmas sweets. Today, some merchants and shopkeepers continue the practice of giving gifts to customers: a bottle of wine, a special loaf of bread, or a big tin of biscuits.

For many years, the Irish have followed the custom of sending Christmas cards. Such cards may have religious themes, in keeping with the holy character of the season. Secular Christmas cards are popular as well and may depict Santa Claus and his reindeer or a snow-covered landscape that is more reminiscent of New England than Ireland. In general, Christmas cards are sent only to relatives and friends who either live some distance away or who will not be coming home for the holiday season. Cards are not sent to neighbors or other people whom the family will be seeing during the holidays.

In Ireland, it is the custom to make Christmas decorations from materials found in the surrounding countryside. A few days before Christmas, the children of the family gather holly and ivy, which grow wild in much of Ireland. Holly with plump red berries is especially sought after. These evergreens are placed on the mantelpiece, around windows, on doors, or around pictures. Loose leaves may be sewn together to make garlands. Bits of greenery may also be stitched to fabric to make seasonal mottoes, such as "Happy Christmas" or "Season's Greetings." In urban areas, the evergreens used to decorate the house are usually purchased. Some families also buy ready-made mottoes, constructed of paper or cardboard, to hang throughout the house. The custom of placing lighted candles in the windows of the home on Christmas Eve originated in Ireland. Today, with increased affluence, many Irish families purchase candleholders to be used for this purpose. In the past, however, few families could afford to buy an item that would be used just once a year. Thus, candleholders were usually fashioned by carving a well in the center of a large turnip (called a rutabaga in the United States). The candle was placed in the well, often with some meal or sand packed around it to ensure that it stood up straight. In some Irish homes, a crock was used in place of a hollowed-out turnip. A circle of colored paper might be fitted over the top of the turnip or crock to disguise its real identity. The children of the family then cut flowers from bits of colored paper that had been saved throughout the past year for this purpose. These paper flowers, along with a sprig of holly or ivy, were used to decorate around the base of the candles. In some parts of Ireland, it was—and still is—customary to place lighted candles in every window of the house. Thus, the making of candleholders often required a great deal of time as well as an ample supply of turnips.

The Nativity scene, also called the crib or the Bethlehem scene, continues to be an essential part of the Christmas observance in most Irish homes. Traditionally, the Nativity scene is set up a few days before Christmas, always in a prominent place in the home. In the past, many people carved the figures in the Bethlehem scene by hand. Today, people usually purchase the Nativity scene, sometimes from Irish craftsmen, who make the figures in the Celtic style. Some families still observe the old custom of saying the rosary each night in front of the Nativity scene. In many Irish homes, the figures of the Three Wise Men are only added to the Bethlehem scene on January 6, the day the Magi are said to have arrived in Bethlehem.

In a Dublin store window, Mother Goose reigns over three men in a tub: the butcher, the baker, and the candlestick maker.

Christmas trees have become popular in Ireland only recently, and most Irish homes have a real tree. On farms, people simply cut down an evergreen on their own property. Most Christmas trees are illuminated with strands of electric lights and include a variety of ornaments. Children often make paper ornaments to hang on the tree. Tinsel is also used. In most Irish homes, the tree is generally put up just a few days before Christmas. In some families, it is customary to decorate the tree on Christmas Eve.

The Christmas season has always been a time when the Irish share with those who are less fortunate. Even the poorer families have always shared what little they had with others. In times past, farmers slaughtered a sheep, cow, or hog just before Christmas. The meat was divided and sent to the families who worked for the farmer, as well as to poor families in the neighborhood. In addition to the meat, the farmer's wife often sent other foods or ingredients needed for a proper Christmas dinner. Some farmers also provided their poorer neighbors with a supply of fuel for the holiday season.

In villages and towns, many housewives cooked two geese or turkeys at Christmas—one for their own family and one to share with less fortunate families. Women also baked extra Christmas cakes to send to families who could not afford such a rich and elaborate treat. The children of the family were often given the job of delivering food to needy neighbors, thus instilling in them the idea that Christmas is, above all, a time for sharing.

In Ireland today, sharing with the poor and the less fortunate continues to be an important part of the observance of Christmas. The Irish are known as generous and charitable people, who believe that "whatever they have is yours." Churches in many areas make an effort to determine who in the parish is truly needy. These families receive Christmas baskets that allow them to have a proper Christmas dinner. Many groups and organizations are involved with charitable activities during the Christmas season. Schoolchildren in Dublin, as well as the rest of Ireland, stage Nativity plays for the benefit of the needy. Groups of carolers representing various organizations sing Christmas hymns in the shopping areas of towns and cities across Ireland. The money collected is given to a variety of charitable causes. Much of the money that is collected by the Wren Boys and mummers' groups on St. Stephen's Day (December 26) is also donated to worthy causes. Wren Boys, like American trick-or-treaters on Halloween, are children who troop door-to-door, usually masked and in costume, chanting rhymes and begging money. Mummers were originally itinerant actors who performed folk plays, always in verse, door-to-door during the Christmas season. Modern mummers usually belong to amateur groups, which stage the traditional plays before an audience. Like the Wren Boys, the mummers generally donate the proceeds from their performances to public charities. In addition to group efforts, individual acts of giving and sharing abound in Ireland during the Christmas season.

The Christmas shopping season in Ireland generally begins a week or two before Christmas, but some people continue the tradition of waiting until Christmas Eve to do all or part of their shopping. The stores do a brisk business during the holiday season, even during poor economic times. Even so, Christmas gifts tend to be less lavish and fewer in number than in the United States. Many Irish people purchase gifts for members of the immediate family

Dublin's luxury shops (above) *offer an extraordinary variety of both domestic and imported goods. Mummers* (left) *stage traditional folk plays during the holiday season. The money raised is usually donated to the needy.*

In Ireland, a white Christmas is rare and is considered an omen of good fortune. But to the children of Dublin, snow simply means a chance to go sledding.

only—those living under the same roof. It is also customary to purchase only one gift for each person on one's Christmas list. The practice of giving multiple gifts for Christmas is uncommon in much of Ireland. In rural areas, Christmas shopping usually means a trip to the nearest village or town. Gifts may also be bought through mail-order catalogs.

The increased affluence in Ireland in recent years has resulted in a greater demand for a wide variety of consumer goods. In Ireland today, it is possible to buy virtually any product from any country in the world. But, in no other Irish city is the range of choice so broad as it is in Dublin, Ireland's capital and largest city. At Christmastime, Dublin offers residents and visitors the charm of an 18th-century Georgian city, but one in which every luxury of the 20th century is available. Smart shops and stores are found up and down Grafton Street, as well as on O'Connell Street and in other parts of the city. These shops and stores display the products of Ireland: Waterford crystal, Belleek chinaware, pottery, jewelry, tweeds, linen, lace, clothing, alcoholic beverages, and an extraordinary variety of handcrafted items. Stores in Dublin also sell an almost unlimited variety of imported goods. Whether domestic or imported, the merchandise offered is usually of the highest quality, not only in Dublin but throughout the country. The Irish prefer quality goods and are willing to spend more for items made to last.

Dublin's many fine stores and shops are gaily decorated for the Christmas season. Father Christmas takes up residence in many stores, spending each day asking good boys and girls what they would like him to leave in their Christmas stockings. Schoolrooms are, of course, decorated by the children, and office buildings, plazas, and hotels are all decked out in Christmas finery. At night, the major shopping streets are illuminated with thousands of twinkling lights. As Christmas approaches, stores may stay open later to accommodate holiday shoppers.

In recent years, hotels in Dublin and other large cities have offered special packages to Christmas guests. These include accommodations, meals, and recreation. Guests generally check in the hotel on December 23 or 24 and stay at least through St. Stephen's Day; some guests remain until New Year's Day. Reservations are essential, as most hotels do not accept drop-in business during Christmas week. Spending Christmas in a hotel provides a welcome change of pace for some families. It also appeals to busy, career-oriented people, who may lack the time to prepare for a traditional Christmas celebration at home, and to people who would otherwise spend Christmas alone. In general, only the more affluent can afford to spend the holidays in a hotel; such accommodations tend to be expensive.

The vast majority of the Irish people, however, continue to celebrate Christmas at home. As in the past, Christmas in Ireland is a time when parents gather their children around them to celebrate both the birth of the Savior and the unity of family life. Unmarried children, even those living in other countries or on other continents, are expected to return home if at all possible. Through the centuries, "home for Christmas" has remained a time-honored Irish tradition. And Ireland is a country where the old traditions are kept and standards are maintained.

In Ireland, children go to see Father Christmas at department stores, just as in the United States they go to see Santa Claus.

comíng home for chrístmas

he traditional Irish Christmas is a celebration of family, but only the immediate family—father, mother, children, and any grandparents or relatives who happen to be living under the same roof. Married children have their own homes and, thus, their own Christmas celebrations. Unmarried children, regardless of age or location, are considered "immediate" and are expected to come home to their parents' in time for Christmas Eve. Distance is no excuse, and every December 24, there is an exodus of sons and daughters traveling out of the cities, out of Cork and Galway, Dublin and even London, back into the countryside.

This "home for Christmas" tradition may remain so strong because Ireland virtually closes up shop from Christmas Day until January 2. On the other hand, it may be that everything is shut down simply because of the demands made by the family at Christmas. In either case, the people of Ireland enjoy a nearly national vacation during the holiday season. Much of Great Britain also slows down during Christmas week, and the many Irish who live and work in England thus have little excuse not to return to the fold.

Many of the Irish who have emigrated to the United States also return for Christmas. But, in the past, when travel was more difficult, the relatives "gone off to America" sent their Christmas greetings via letter, what the Irish call the "American letter." These letters became a very important fixture of Christmas in Ireland. Enclosed with the news of family and their wishes for a "happy Christmas" was, invariably, a gift of cash. For the nearly one hundred years between the potato famine and the end of World War II, this money enabled thousands of Irish families to enjoy a "good and proper" Christmas, to buy the children gifts and to put meat on the table for Christmas Day. Today, the Irish still expect to hear from their relatives living in the United States. But in most cases, the "American letters" no longer contain the gifts of cash, simply because most Irish families no longer need financial help.

Today, as in the past, people are up early on Christmas Eve, for there is much to be done to prepare for the Christmas celebration. Although the decorations may have been weeks in the making, they may not be set into place until Christmas Eve. In some families, it is traditional to put up the Christmas tree on this day. Christmas Eve also is an important shopping day in much of Ireland. Some people do most or even all of their shopping on December 24, which is not as impossible as it sounds given the relatively small number of gifts that most people purchase. In much of Ireland, shops stay open later than usual on the Eve to accommodate the last-minute rush. Stores may even offer bargains to attract Christmas Eve shoppers. Many merchants and shopkeepers also give gifts to their regular customers on Christmas Eve—a bottle of wine, a box of Christmas sweets, or a special loaf of bread.

Many employees are off by midday on Christmas Eve. Some stop off at the pub for a pint or two before returning home, and many pubs in Ireland continue the tradition of offering free drinks to their patrons on Christmas Eve. Once family members return home, they usually help with the last-minute Christmas preparations—the final cleaning and tidying, putting the last touches on the decorations, and preparing the food for the Christmas Day dinner. On the farm, the Christmas goose or turkey must be killed, plucked, and dressed for cooking.

In Ireland, Christmas Eve was, traditionally, a fast day. People ate nothing until the main meal of the day, which was meatless. Dinner on Christmas Eve was always simple—fish, served with a white sauce and potatoes, or fish stew or soup served with vegetables. Potato soup was also a common main dish on Christmas Eve. In a custom that resembled the patriarchal division of the Paschal lamb at the Jewish Passover Seder, the man of the house personally boiled and peeled the potatoes for the soup. He then sliced them into soup plates half filled with spiced, warm milk, carefully dividing the potatoes equally between the members of the family. Many people still fast and abstain from eating meat on Christmas Eve as a private act of devotion, and throughout the country, dinner remains simple.

The old Irish custom of placing lighted candles in the windows of the house is still observed. At nightfall on Christmas Eve, a tall, thick candle is set in the principal window of the house, often by the father of the family. The candle may be either white, red, blue, or green and is often two feet in height. Traditionally, the honor of lighting the main candle belonged to the youngest child or to a daughter named Mary. Many families place a candle in every window of the house, or at least, in all of the front windows. According to custom, all candles must be lighted from the principal candle.

There is always a great excitement as the children of the family rush from window to window to see the effect of the lighted candles. Invariably, they then run out into the garden or street to see how each window looks from the outside. The next step is to examine the windows of all the adjoining houses, to make sure that all neighbors have done their "duty." It was once held that anyone who did not illuminate his or her windows could not be a Christian. "Fall down on your knees," the mother of the family would exclaim upon being told that no candles were flickering through the windows of a certain house. The custom of viewing the whole countryside from the top of a hill on

On Christmas Eve, train and bus stations (left) are filled with people on their way home for the holiday. A rural postman (below) delivers Christmas mail, which may include an "American letter." Holiday greetings from relatives in the United States have become a Christmas tradition in Ireland.

Christmas Eve is still practiced by many Irish families today. Once it is completely dark, parents take their children to the nearest high point to marvel at the fairyland of twinkling lights. Undoubtedly, the dozens of flickering candles looked even more beautiful in the days before electricity, when their glow provided the only illumination in the dark countryside.

In many homes, the lighting of the candles is accompanied by a brief ceremony or, at the very least, a prayer. This is done lest people forget the original political and religious significance of the custom. Lighted candles were first placed in windows on Christmas Eve during the English rule of Ireland. Under Protestant Great Britain, Ireland's Catholics were persecuted for their religious beliefs. Priests were forbidden to say Mass, although many continued to celebrate the Mass in secret. Thus, on Christmas Eve, the holiest night of the year, the Catholic faithful put lighted candles in their windows as a signal to passing priests that their's was a "safe" house, one in which Mass could be celebrated without fear of reprisal.

When the British authorities inquired about this practice, they were told that the candles served as a light to guide the path of Joseph and Mary. The Irish explained that Joseph and Mary wander the world every Christmas Eve looking for a place to stay, just as they did in Bethlehem so many years ago. The candles served as a sign that the travelers were welcome to take refuge. For the most part, the British authorities allowed the practice to continue, attributing it to "Irish superstition."

Many of the faithful did, in fact, believe that the Holy Family might visit their home on Christmas Eve. In addition to placing lighted candles in the windows, some families made more elaborate preparations in case the weary travelers should stop. Before retiring for the night, the floor was swept and the

Christmas Eve shoppers (opposite page) *fill the streets of Dublin on this traditional shopping day. The Christmas tree* (below) *is a relatively new custom in Ireland. In many houses, the tree, like the candle in the window, is not lit until dusk on Christmas Eve.*

fire banked. The table was set for three, and food and a lighted candle were left on the table. Throughout Ireland, doors were left unlatched; some were left wide open, just in case. A dish of water was placed on the windowsill for the Holy Family to bless; the water was then kept throughout the year and used for curing illnesses.

In the not-too-distant past, the celebration of Christmas began with the lighting of the candles on Christmas Eve. The good dishes were brought out in honor of this holiest night of the year. The rich Christmas cake was cut, and tea, sherry, and punch were served along with puddings and other treats. There was music, and around the fireplace hearth, there was storytelling. There are many tales and legends associated with this one night of the year, legends that are strangely interwoven with the idea of, and preparations for, the Holy Family's wanderings on Christmas Eve. Around the glow of the fire, the old passed on to the young superstitions concerning the spirits of the dead, which were said to roam about the land on Christmas Eve. The fire was banked, food was left on the table, and the door was unlatched not only for the Holy Family, but also for the benefit of the spirits of ancestors who, like the living family, "came home" for Christmas. Because the spirits of all of the dead roamed on this night, it was not wise to be out and about after dark on December 24, and farmers, traditionally, came in from the fields by midday.

Christmas Eve was, however, an excellent night on which to die, for the gates of heaven were open to everyone on the eve of Christ's birth. God answered all prayers offered up on Christmas Eve as well. It was thought that the Devil died annually on December 24, and church bells, throughout Ireland, tolled for the hour before midnight to mark his funeral.

There were many other legends and tales told around the waning light of countless peat fires on Christmas Eve. The houses and churches of Ireland were decorated for Christmas with holly because on this night an angel sprang from every spike and danced in attendance to the Christ child. And in the barnyards, the animals—the cows and horses and pigs—were blessed for a single hour with the gift of speech and knelt in prayer and worship of the Infant. Now, to check this miracle out for oneself was the very proof that one was a disbeliever, and besides, it was, as everyone knew, foolish indeed to go out in the cold, damp air of the Eve.

Even the rooster, out in the yard, was aware of the significance of this one night of the year. Filled with the joy of Christmas, he was known to crow throughout the night. To hear the cock crow on the stroke of midnight was a particularly good omen.

Of course, the Irish no longer believe in the old legends, no matter how much they might enjoy retelling them. But old habits die hard, and certain bits of the past linger on. Throughout the country, businesses and factories close at noon on December 24. Ireland is a relatively small island, 289 miles long and 177 miles wide; thus, everyone has the opportunity to be home before dark. And the unmarried sons and daughters of Ireland do still return to the warm, safe circle of the family on Christmas Eve. It's a pleasant custom that has been going on for so long that no one remembers just how it started.

Today, many people complete their Christmas Eve celebrations by attending Midnight Mass. This is a relatively new tradition in Ireland, as the custom of

It is the custom for a daughter named Mary or for the youngest child of the house to light the candles on Christmas Eve.

the country was "First Light" Mass—the celebration of Mass at the first light of dawn on Christmas morning. People went to church on Christmas Eve, traditionally, for confession only. In the past, mothers assumed the duty of urging every member of the family to make confession sometime during the day, with reminders beginning well in advance of the 24th of December. Going to confession was very much a part of the penitential character of the Advent season, part of the spiritual preparation for Christ's coming. It was once a common sight on Christmas Eve for the lines of people, waiting to make their confessions, to stretch out the doors of the churches. Although many people in Ireland still go to confession on this day, changes in Church law have made this a less universal custom of the season.

Midnight Mass, except in rural areas, is now considered by many Irish people to be an essential part of the Christmas celebration, and huge crowds attend the late services in churches throughout the country. Midnight Mass in the Catholic Church in Ireland is quite similar to Mass on other occasions, except that the readings, sermon, and music all focus on the miracle of Christ's birth. The Mass celebrates the birth of the Savior sent by a loving God to redeem the souls of all sinners. Three hymns are traditionally sung: "Silent Night," "Angels in the Realms of Glory" (*Gloria in Excelsis Deo*), and "Adeste Fidelis" sung in Latin.

Before leaving church after Midnight Mass, it is essential to wish one's neighbors and friends a *"Nodlaig Nait Cugat,"* Happy Christmas in Gaelic. The family then starts for home, perhaps walking so that they may enjoy the sight of all the candles in the windows.

It is quite late when they reach home, and the children, who hung up their stockings before going to Mass, are put to bed. The Christmas stockings that Irish children hang up today may be specially made or purchased for this purpose. But in the past, most children simply hung one of their own stockings from the foot of their beds. It was always the biggest stocking they could find, the better to accommodate all their hopes for Christmas morning.

If the family holds to this tradition of hanging the stockings from the bedsteads, the parents must remain up long enough to ensure that all the children are soundly asleep before the gifts can be put in place. Then there are the candles to be put out, and the door to be locked. But throughout Ireland, there are still houses where the candles are left burning through the night, houses where the doors are left unlatched. And a plate of something—cookies or pudding—is left on the table, with the light in that room left burning. It is simply the tradition.

a savior
is born

Christmas Day in Ireland is a quiet day. With the exception of the churches, everything is closed—restaurants, pubs, cinemas, shops. It is a family day, spent at home. The unannounced visits between friends and relatives, which are so much a part of life on this sociable island, are rare on Christmas. Everyone understands: Christmas is family, and only immediate family at that.

In most Irish houses, the day begins early. Adults who do not awaken naturally are soon roused by the squeals of delight that accompany the children's "rush to the socks." Excited shouts fill the air as the gifts and treats left by Father Christmas, or Santa Claus, are discovered in the stockings. Father Christmas, or Santa, has been known, when visiting Irish homes with a goodly number of children, to arrange the gifts on chairs, each chair labeled with a child's name; this, of course, prevents the collisions that may result when five or six "wee ones" all dive at the same time for the same pile of packages. After the contents of the stockings are revealed, older family members may then gather around the Christmas tree, a rather new tradition in Ireland, to exchange their Christmas gifts. Although the exchange of presents has become more lavish in Ireland in recent years, gifts still tend to be fewer and simpler than in many other countries. People remember the "hard times" all too well.

In times past, the Irish had little money to spend on Christmas, and presents tended to be very practical—a pair of socks, a shirt, a new pair of shoes. Irish children who found an orange in their stocking considered it a great treat; fresh fruit was rare in the winter months. In addition to fruit, children were given nuts, candy, or homemade sweets. Depending upon the family finances, children may have received a storybook or small toy, perhaps a top with a string or a penny doll. Such gifts were highly prized. As recently as twenty years ago, a bicycle was considered a lavish gift for a child. As the Irish have become more affluent, Christmas gifts have become less practical. Television, a relatively new import to Ireland, has also begun to change consumer buying habits. But Christmas continues to be primarily a religious and family celebration. The commercial aspects of the holiday are still secondary in importance.

In rural areas, many people still attend Mass on Christmas morning rather than at midnight on Christmas Eve. The first Mass may be said as early as six o'clock, although eight o'clock is the more customary time. In the past, when people walked to church, it was necessary to leave home before daybreak. Lanterns and torches were carried to light the way. Many Irish people vividly recall Christmas morning in those days before electricity or cars were common to the countryside. Families, setting out for church in the dark, were cheered and warmed along the way by the sight of candles still burning in the windows of their neighbors' houses. Through the doorways left open in case family spirits should need shelter on Christmas Eve, they greeted their friends all up the lane with "Happy Christmas."

"First Light" Mass is much the same as Midnight Mass on Christmas Eve, a joyous reminder to the faithful of Christ's birth. In Ireland, a second and third Mass are usually said on Christmas morning. In the past, it was common for people to stay for all three Masses, believing that God would reward such an act of devotion. Special prayers before the church Nativity scene, either before or after Mass, were an additional act of devotion that might merit extra days of indulgence.

When Mass ends, most families go home for the rest of the day, but not before wishing *Nodlaig Nait Cugat*—Happy Christmas in Gaelic, the native language of Ireland—to one and all. The men and boys of the family then begin the Christmas games, either hurling, which resembles field hockey, or Gaelic football, which is similar to soccer. In the past, hurling matches often began right outside the church gate. Men took their hurleys, or sticks, with them to church so that no time would be lost in getting the match started. In some parts of Ireland, people held shooting competitions on Christmas Day. Hunting hares with greyhounds is still a popular Christmas sport in some counties.

hile the men of the family are out playing, the women are busy preparing the feast, traditionally the most elaborate meal of the year. As always, the focus is on fresh, wholesome foods prepared simply, but with great care. Potatoes and other vegetables continue to be the staples of the Irish diet; and freshly baked bread, served with jam or marmalade, is still served with every meal. In farming areas, much of the food that appears on the Christmas table is raised or grown at home, from the goose or turkey to the potatoes, carrots, peas, and other vegetables.

The Christmas table is set with the best the family can muster: a linen or lace tablecloth; good china; silver that has been polished until it gleams; and cut-glass stemware. The holiday table reflects the pride the Irish have in their homes and the pleasure they take in life's refinements. Even the poorest Irish family owns a set of china to use on Christmas and other special occasions. The good dishes may stay in the back of the cupboard, or the chest or dresser as it is called in Ireland, but they are always ready to be used should visitors drop in. In the humblest home, food is always served to guests on a tablecloth, freshly laundered and neatly pressed.

In Ireland, Christmas is a day of charity, and before partaking of the

Christmas feast, many Irish families see to the needs of less fortunate neighbors. The children of the family are often assigned the task of delivering gifts of food or ingredients for a "proper" dinner to people in the neighborhood. On Christmas Day, children are out delivering platefuls of food, "piping hot," to neighbors and friends unable to do their own cooking. Only then does the family sit down to its own Christmas dinner, usually at one or two o'clock in the afternoon. In cities, Christmas dinner may be served as late as three o'clock.

The traditional Irish Christmas feast includes roast goose or turkey. In many homes, the bird is served with a large slice of ham under it. In Ireland, the traditional stuffing for the bird is potato, heavily seasoned with black pepper. Potatoes, either mashed or roasted, are also served with the meal, as is gravy for pouring over the meat and sometimes the dressing. One or two vegetable dishes, such as minted peas or glazed carrots, may also be served. Some people begin the meal with soup, perhaps beef broth. Applesauce or gooseberry sauce may also be served with the goose and ham.

Once the main courses of the meal have been eaten, a dazzling array of Christmas desserts appear. Some of the desserts, the Christmas cake and puddings, for example, were made weeks before to allow time for "mellowing." The Christmas cake, known as the "cake of the year," contains only the finest fruits, nuts, raisins, and spices. The Christmas puddings are made with equal care. Both bread and plum pudding are traditional Christmas treats. Both may be served with toppings, such as custard, butterscotch, brandy, or hard sauce.

Before serving plum pudding, many Irish cooks ignite whiskey or brandy and pour it over the pudding. Other cooks pour the whiskey or brandy over the pudding and then set it aflame. In some homes, at least three puddings are made for the holiday season: one for Christmas, one for New Year's, and one for Twelfth Night, January 6. Other special Christmas treats are mincemeat pies or tarts, sherry trifle, soda scones, fairy cake, and cookies.

A big pot of tea is brewed to serve with the Christmas desserts. The Irish are every bit as fond of their tea as the British. Dinner is always followed by at least one cup of tea, "to wash down the spuds." In most Irish homes, "a cup of the pot" is ready to be poured at any time of the day. Tea time is observed even in the fields, with farmers' wives delivering a jug of hot tea to their husbands.

Turkey or goose was not always the traditional main course on Christmas Day. Spiced beef was once very popular for Christmas dinner. This was prepared by rubbing a joint of beef with a spice mixture and then allowing it to stand in the mixture for a week. The beef was then boiled in water over a bed of vegetables. In certain Irish counties, boiled ox head was traditional fare on Christmas Day. In the past, few people in Ireland could afford to eat meat more than once a week, usually on Sunday. Dinner during the rest of the week consisted mainly of bread, potatoes, and cabbage. A Christmas dinner that included any kind of meat was, thus, considered a great treat.

Today, as in the past, family members generally stay home after completing their Christmas feast. Candles are lit, as they are on Christmas Eve, and placed in the windows where the flicker of the light plays against the old, hand-rolled glass. The rest of the evening is spent relaxing around the hearth, the warmth of the fire. Family members may talk, sing, or play musical instruments. And if the family is lucky, and most Irish families are lucky in this way, someone has a talent for telling stories. The stories are not new. Everyone has heard them all before. But no one minds because, in Ireland, storytelling is an art that is passed on, like the stories themselves, from the old to the young, from generation to generation.

Men and boys play Gaelic football, a game similar to soccer, while the women of the family prepare Christmas dinner.

Christmas dinner (above) begins with a prayer of thanksgiving. Over a late afternoon cup of tea and a second helping of dessert (left), the stories of life in Ireland are passed from the old to the young.

sing holly, sing ivy

n Ireland, the Christmas season can be divided into two distinct halves. The first half, the weeks of Advent and Christmas Eve and Day, are primarily spiritual, a celebration of church and family. The second half of the season, the twelve days of Christmas, December 26 to January 6, are, for the most part, just for fun. And the fun begins early on the "first day of Christmas," which is St. Stephen's Day.

St. Stephen's Day honors the first Christian martyr, who was accused of speaking against the laws of Moses and stoned shortly after the Crucifixion of Christ. In Ireland, St. Stephen's Day is a national holiday, celebrated with great relish. However, the celebration has little or nothing to do with the first saint. For hundreds of years, December 26 has been the day of the "Wren Boys." "Hunting the wren" or "going on the wren" is a peculiar custom, similar to Halloween, that survives on the Isle of Man, in part of Spain, and throughout Ireland. Originally, hunting the wren began a day or two before Christmas or even on Christmas night; small bands of boys eagerly peered into bushes and under the eaves of houses for the tiny wren bird. Once a wren was spotted, the boys chased the hapless bird until it was either caught or dropped from exhaustion. The dead bird was tied to the top of a holly bush or to the end of a wooden pole. The bush or pole was then decorated with ribbons and bits of colored paper.

Early in the morning of St. Stephen's Day, the boys gathered to "go on the wren." The bird attached to the bush or pole was carried around by the band of boys, who were always disguised in some form. Straw masks were worn, or faces were blackened with burnt cork. It was common for the boys to dress up in old clothes, usually women's dresses, which were saved through the year for this purpose. The boys carried the bird from house to house in the neighborhood, knocking on doors and begging, sometimes demanding, admittance. Once inside the house, they danced and played instruments—melodeons, accordions, tambourines, drums, or horns. All would then favor the household with some version of the Wren Boys' song:

> The wren, the wren, the king of all birds,
> St. Stephen's Day was caught in the furze,
> Although he is little, his family is great,
> I pray you, good landlady, give us a treat.

Although some families gave the Wren Boys food, the requested treat was usually money or drink. If a contribution was not forthcoming after one verse, the boys were more than happy to sing another:

> My box would speak, if it had but a tongue,
> And two or three shillings would do it not wrong,
> Sing holly, sing ivy—sing ivy, sing holly,
> A drop just to drink, it would drown melancholy.

A third verse of the Wren Boys' song warns about the size of the contribution:

> And if you draw it of the best,
> I hope in heaven your soul will rest;
> But if you draw it of the small,
> It won't agree with these Wren Boys at all.

The person who contributed his or her "fair share" was often given a feather plucked from the wren; this was believed to bring good luck. The Wren Boys were then off to the next house, dancing, playing their instruments, and singing their verses all over again. It was the custom to stop at every village house, except those in which a death had occurred during the previous year. If, in fact, the Wren Boys failed to stop at a particular house, the head of the family might take great offense. Similarly, the Wren Boys might take great offense if a family refused their request for money. Retribution consisted of burying what was left of the wren in front of the house that failed to contribute. This was believed to bring bad luck to the offending party.

The Wren Boys would often continue making their rounds until dark. Some of the more energetic groups might cover a stretch of nine or ten miles, singing and dancing at virtually every house along the way. The money collected by the various groups was often used to buy food and drink for a party or dance held later on St. Stephen's Night. The entire neighborhood was invited to the party, although an admission fee was charged to those who had not "gone on the wren." Wren Dances were, sometimes, held on the night after St. Stephen's, as the boys were too tired to dance after their long day.

Irish historians offer several explanations for the origin of the custom of hunting the wren on St. Stephen's Day. According to one legend, St. Stephen was hiding from enemies in a bush. A wren betrayed his whereabouts with its noisy chattering. Thus, the wren was hunted on St. Stephen's Day and stoned, like St. Stephen, with pebbles and sticks.

Another legend, dating from the late 700's when the Vikings were invading Ireland, holds that Irish soldiers were betrayed by a wren as they were sneaking up on sleeping Viking raiders. The wren began to eat breadcrumbs left on the head of a Viking drum. The rat-a-tat-tat of the bird's pecking on the skin of the

An 1852 English engraving of Irish Wren Boys.

drum woke the drummer boy, who sounded the alarm. The Irish soldiers were defeated by the Vikings, and the hapless wren has been persecuted for its treachery ever since.

The hunting of the wren has also been connected to the pagan custom of sacrificing a sacred symbol at year's end. This explanation probably comes closest to the truth. Pagan symbols of the winter solstice are interwoven with Christian symbols of Christmas throughout Europe; in Great Britain, for example, dead robins are still occasionally pictured on Christmas cards and decorations. In Ireland, the wren has, traditionally, been revered and accorded a place of honor as the "king of birds." An ancient Irish folk tale describes a contest staged among all the birds to decide which should be named king. The honor would go to the bird who could fly the highest. Each bird, in turn, did his best, but the eagle soared higher than the rest. But victory was snatched from the proud eagle when the little wren, who had been hiding on the eagle's back, suddenly appeared and flew higher still. Thus, it was the clever wren, not the mighty eagle, who was proclaimed "king of all the birds."

In certain parts of Ireland, "going on the wren" became quite elaborate. Imitating mummers' plays in some respects, the Wren Boys assumed particular characters and presented skits. One boy would play the part of an Irish chieftain, who might be named after the most prominent family in the neighborhood. Another boy would play the role of "Sir Sop," an English chieftain. The parts of servants and officers in attendance to the two chieftains were played by the other boys. The Irish chieftain, of course, was well dressed, while Sir Sop was clothed in straw with a matching straw helmet. The Wren Boys acted out the skit at each house, interspersing the dialogue with songs and dances.

In another version of "going on the wren," a wooden hobbyhorse was used. Similar to the hodening horse used in holiday games in England and Wales, the contraption consisted of a carved horse's head with dangling legs. The wooden frame, which was draped with a white sheet, was carried on the shoulders of a single Wren Boy. Woe be to anyone who either got too close to the horse or who did not treat the group with sufficient money. The beast was equipped with movable jaws and back legs that were controlled, from within, with cords. The horse could, thus, snap with its jaws or kick with its hind legs.

"Going on the wren" had, by the turn of this century, fallen into disrepute. Adults, whom the "respectable folk" considered the town rabble, dressed up on St. Stephen's Day and descended upon their neighbors, loudly demanding money and drink. As the day wore on, the crowds in the streets became rowdy. Many people condemned the entire custom as simply an excuse for loud, drunken behavior. Parents forbade their children to go out at all, seeing it as simply a form of begging. Of course, boys would sneak off despite their parents' objections, taking care to be home, all cleaned up, by the midday meal.

The custom of "going on the wren" has been revived in modern times. Of course, in some parts of the country, especially rural areas, the tradition never completely died out. Happily, the wren is no longer hunted or killed for this purpose. A straw wren, a toy bird, or a bunch of feathers is, instead, fastened to the top of a holly bush. In some parts of Ireland, a live bird is taken around in a cage. Today, many of the Wren Boys are actually adults, and girls are now welcome to join in the fun. The money collected is usually donated to charity or used to finance civic, community, or school projects. Some Wren Boys buy athletic equipment or add the money to funds being raised for the construction of a playing field. And, of course, Wren Dances continue to be held throughout Ireland.

The costumes of the modern-day Wren Boys are no less elaborate than those worn in the past. Many of the boys and young men continue to dress as women, and the girls, who now go on the wren, disguise themselves as boys. Faces are still blackened with burnt cork, and strange masks continue to be made from straw. The groups go from house to house, although the rounds

With elaborate costumes and traditional folk dances, modern Wren Boys (and girls) continue the customs of St. Stephen's Day. The man on the far left of the photograph carries the "bush" in which the symbolic wren nests.

are usually made a little later in the morning than they once were. In some areas, groups of Wren Boys rent buses to take them from town to town throughout the day. As in the past, the Wren Boys dance and play musical instruments in addition to singing or chanting the Wren Song, which has changed very little with time:

> The wren, the wren, the king of all birds,
> On St. Stephen's Day, was caught in the furze;
> Though his body is small, his family is great,
> So if you please, your honor, give us a treat.
>
> On Christmas Day I turned a spit;
> I burned my finger: I feel it yet,
> Up with the kettle, and down with the pan:
> Give us some money to bury the wren.

Mummers' plays are traditionally staged on St. Stephen's Day and throughout the twelve days of Christmas. In Ireland, mummers are often called Christmas Rhymers, and the dialogue of the play is always recited in verse:

> Room, room, brave gallant boys
> Give us room to rhyme
> To show a bit of our activity
> At the Christmas time . . .

Although mumming is an import from Great Britain, Irish mummers' plays have a distinctly nationalistic flavor and are an important part of the nation's folk culture. The plots of the plays are simple and usually revolve around a duel between two great heroes. One of the heroes takes a "fall," but is miraculously cured by "the Doctor." The characters in Irish mummers' plays spring, for the most part, from Irish and English history. The heroes are usually

Groups of mummers and folk dancers (right) perform in the streets of Dublin on December 26, St. Stephen's Day. On this day, professional hurling matches (below) attract huge crowds.

saints—St. Patrick or even England's St. George. The villains are usually English rulers who were hard on the Irish—Oliver Cromwell or King William III. Other characters—Father Christmas, Beelzebub, the Devil, the Doctor, and even the Wren—are mixed in to keep the plot moving, to sing the narrative, or, perhaps, just for fun.

The characters in the mummers' plays wear elaborate costumes and sing and play musical instruments whenever possible. Spirited and intricate dances, complete with swinging swords, are also performed.

Today, most mummers' plays are staged before groups in halls or theaters, or even on television. In the past, however, troupes of mummers traveled from house to house, offering their verses and songs in the form of good wishes for a happy Christmas and a prosperous New Year:

> God bless the master of this house
> Likewise the mistress too
> May their barns be filled with wheat and corn
> And their hearts be always true.
> A merry Christmas is our wish
> Where'er we do appear
> To you a well-filled purse, a well-filled dish
> And a happy, bright New Year.

Not everyone, of course, spends St. Stephen's Day "going on the wren" or

The famous Christmas Dog Show is held at the Royal Dublin Society Grounds on St. Stephen's Day.

Steeplechasing (above) *and fox hunting* (opposite page) *are traditional St. Stephen's Day events. The Irish love horses, and horses seemingly love Ireland. The combination of a relatively mild climate and limestone-based pastures produces horses that are world-famous for their ability, stamina, and courage.*

performing with a band of mummers. On December 26, the front door is open, not only to the Wren Boys, but to one and all. And throughout the country, friends are out paying calls, dropping in next door for a chat, a cup of tea, and a peek at what Father Christmas, or Santa, brought the neighbors. It is a day to relax and simply recover from the efforts and excesses of Christmas Day. It was, in the past, customary to fast on St. Stephen's Day. The Irish believed that giving up food on December 26 would ensure good health throughout the rest of the year. It has been suggested, however, that fasting on St. Stephen's Day was simply a natural consequence of overindulging on Christmas Day.

St. Stephen's Day is an important sporting day throughout Ireland. Crowds flock to the race tracks for both horse and greyhound racing. Hurling and Gaelic football games, both amateur and professional, are well attended. In some areas of the country, competitions between school basketball teams are held in community centers. Fishing, especially for salmon, and hunting, or beagling and fowling, as it is sometimes called in Ireland, are popular post-Christmas activities. One of the major dog shows of the year is held on St. Stephen's Day. And in this country famous for its horses, there is fox hunting, complete with traditional "pinks" and Master of Foxhounds. In the past, cockfighting and bull-baiting were also favored events in some parts of the country.

On St. Stephen's Night there is only one activity worth mentioning—dancing. All across Ireland, in nearly every village and town, there is a hall for dancing, and thanks to the Wren Boys and the shillings donated by the neighbors, on this night every hall is filled to capacity.

the twelve days of christmas

The twelve days of Christmas—the interval between Christmas Day and Twelfth-night or Epiphany—is an important part of the holiday season in Ireland. The Irish, initially, enjoy a vacation during either part or all of the twelve-day period. The entire nation relaxes and enjoys the less serious holiday events that follow Christmas Day. St. Stephen's Day, filled with the fun of "going on the wren," mumming, and country dances, is, of course, the first of the twelve days. The second major event of the period is Holy Innocents' Day. Many people attend Mass on December 28 to commemorate the slaughter of the male children of Bethlehem. King Herod, believing a Messiah destined to become the new "King of the Jews" had been born, decreed that all male children under the age of two be put to the sword. Joseph, warned by an angel, saved the Infant Jesus by fleeing to Egypt.

In Ireland, Holy Innocents' Day was thought to be filled with bad omens. It was referred to as "the cross day of the year," *Lá Crostna na Bliana* in Gaelic. On *Lá Crostna na Bliana*, the winds of fate blew cross, or ill-tempered, in memory of the senseless slaughter of children. No new enterprises were begun in Ireland on December 28. In some counties, people refused to transact any business. It was believed that the ill omens associated with the day extended throughout the year. Thus, if Holy Innocents fell on a Thursday, all Thursdays throughout the year were unlucky, and no business could be successfully transacted on that day of the week. The Irish, of course, no longer consider Holy Innocents' Day so fraught with danger. But the slaughter of innocent children is still remembered with prayers and church services.

The next important event of the twelve days of Christmas is, of course, New Year's Eve and Day. The Irish have a somewhat ambivalent attitude about New Year's. The younger generation has begun to celebrate the event in a distinctly different fashion than the older generation. New Year's was not considered a holiday in Ireland until the government, in recent years, declared it one.

51

And since the government decreed that everyone has the first day of the year off, the younger generation has, naturally, begun to party on New Year's Eve. Pubs, lounges, and nightclubs are now filled on December 31. In cities, there are bonfires and parades in anticipation of midnight. Fireworks are set off and church bells are rung to mark the first minutes of the new year.

In Ireland, the customary way to note the passing of the old year was to eat a heavy meal on New Year's Eve. The meal was to guard against hunger in the coming year. New Year's Eve, which in Gaelic is called *Oíche Coille,* thus, became known as "the night of the big portion," or *Oíche na Coda Móire.* In some areas of the country, it was believed that every bit of food in the house had to be eaten before January 1. This was to ensure plenty in the following months.

A variety of New Year's Eve customs evolved around the theme of keeping hunger at bay. In some sections of Ireland, the man of the house, armed with a cake or a loaf of bread, struck the inside of the door three times saying:

> Out with misfortune, in with happiness,
> from tonight to this night twelve months,
> in the name of the Father, and of the Son,
> and of the Holy Ghost, Amen.

In another variation, it was the woman of the house who took up the cake to ensure plenty, saying three times:

> We warn famine to retire
> To the country of the Turks;
> From this night to this night, twelvemonth,
> And even this very night.

In yet another version of this ritual, the cake was thrown against the outside of the main door of the house. And in the countryside, to ensure an ample supply of food for the farm animals, a cake was thrown at the barn doors.

There was a time when the Irish carefully studied the weather on New Year's Eve. Weather conditions on the last night of the year were thought to be a harbinger of weather conditions through the following twelve months. The weather was also held to be an omen of political fortunes as well. A wind that blew from the west on New Year's Eve was interpreted as a sign that the Irish cause, that is, the struggle for independence, would flourish; a wind that blew from the east was, on the other hand, viewed as an indication that English rule would continue for another twelve months.

Spinsters and girls of marriageable age traditionally placed ivy and holly leaves under their pillows on New Year's Eve. The leaves were thought to induce dreams of the man a girl was fated to marry. Before falling asleep, the girl whispered into her pillow:

> Oh, ivy green and holly red,
> Tell, tell whom I shall wed!

In the northern counties of Ireland, children once went door-to-door on New Year's Day, carrying bundles of straw. At each door the child presented the lady of the house with a wisp of straw and was, in return, rewarded with a penny or two. The significance of this custom seems to be lost in time.

It is not so difficult, however, to understand the motives behind most Irish New Year's customs if one considers the extraordinary hardships that the Irish have endured, especially during the time of the famine. It is also not difficult

Irish families often wait until January 6, the Feast of the Epiphany, to place the Three Wise Men in the Nativity scene. This set was made in County Tipperary of native hardwoods.

to understand why the old may view the younger generation's New Year's celebrations as "tempting the fates." There is, however, one New Year custom that has passed from the old to the young, "first footing." Dark-haired men and boys are still much in demand on New Year's Day. The Irish, like the Scots, believe that luck comes to a house when the first person to step over the threshold on New Year's Day is a man with dark hair and fair features.

In Ireland, the first Monday of the new year is referred to as Handsel Monday. On this day, the children are again out knocking on their neighbors' doors, soliciting a handsel, which is a small gift of money. It was once considered very unlucky to refuse a child a handsel, and adults often tried to accrue better luck for the coming year by presenting the child with a coin before actually being asked for it. In some counties of Ireland, it was the practice to offer the children small, sweet cakes, instead of coins. The cakes were baked especially for the day by housewives, which may explain why the day is also referred to as Goodwives' Day.

The Christmas season in Ireland officially ends on January 6 with the Feast of the Epiphany. This day commemorates the adoration of the Magi. The Epiphany, also called "Twelfth-night" or "Little Christmas," was once considered nearly as important as Christmas Day and was, until recent years, a national holiday in Ireland. Although no longer obliged to do so, many Irish continue to attend Mass on the Epiphany, the day the Three Wise Men are believed to have arrived before the Infant Jesus. The Irish speak of Twelfth-night as a day of sadness; because the Christmas season is the most joyous time of the year, the last day of the season is always melancholy.

In Ireland, the Epiphany is sometimes called "women's Christmas." And it was once customary to serve a smaller and more "feminine" version of the Christmas Day meal. Instead of whiskey and beef or goose, sherry and tea and "dainties" were offered. This is no longer universally done, but the custom of placing candles in the windows on Twelfth-night is still practiced throughout the country. Many people put three candles in the window to represent the Three Wise Men. In the past, people anchored one candle in a tall sieve of oats. Twelve smaller candles were then arranged around the large candle. This represented Christ, the light of the world, surrounded by the twelve apostles.

Candles were also used on Twelfth-night for another ritual. Each member of a family was assigned a candle, which he or she placed on a cake and then lighted. The family stood around the cake, watching the order in which the candles burned out. It was held that the order indicated the order in which the family members would die.

The Irish take down their Christmas decorations on January 7. The tree, holly, and other greenery are discarded. In the past, it was traditional to burn the Christmas greens, as it was considered bad luck to simply put them on a trash heap. Permanent decorations, the ornaments, lights, and Nativity scene, are carefully wrapped and stored away for next Christmas. Although the season has ended, much of the spirit of Christmas in Ireland—the keen interest in preserving the country's history, customs, and traditions; the maintenance of religious and family life; and the charity and concern for the poor and disadvantaged—continues, reinforced throughout the year by the memory of *Nodlaig Nait Cugat.*

The sight of twinkling lights and the sounds of church bells pull Dubliners into the streets on New Year's Eve.

54

the wee christmas cabin of carn-na-ween

by Ruth Sawyer

hundred years ago and more, on a stretch of road that runs from the town of Donegal to Killybegs and the sea, a drove of tinkers went their way of mending pots and thieving lambs. Having a child too many for the caravan, they left it, newborn, upon a cabin doorsill in Carn-na-ween.

The cabin belonged to Bridget and Conal Hegarty. Now these two had little wish for another child, having childher aplenty of their own; but they could not leave the wee thing to die at their door, nor had they a mind to throw it into the turf pit. So Bridget suckled it with her own wean; she divided the cradle between them. And in time she came to love it as her own and fought its battles when the neighbors would have cursed it for a tinker's child.

I am forgetting to tell you that the child was a girl and Bridget named her Oona. She grew into the prettiest, the gentlest-mannered lass in all the county. Bridget did her best to get the lads to court her, forever pointing out how clever she was with her needle, how sweet her voice when she lilted an air, the sure way she had of making bannock, broth, or jam.

But the lads would have none of her. Marry a tinker's child? Never! Their feet might be itching to take her to a crossroad's dance, their arms hungering to be holding her, but they kept the width of a cabin or the road always between her and them. Aye, there was never a chance came to Oona to marry and have childher of her own, or a cabin she could call hers.

All of Bridget and Conal's lasses married; but Oona stayed on to mind the house for them, to care for them through their sicknesses, to help them gently into their graves. I think from the beginning Oona had a dream—a dream that, having cared lovingly for the old, someone would be leaving her, at long last, a cabin for her own keeping. Bridget, before she died, broke the dream at its beginning. "The cabin goes to Michael," she said. "He and his young wife will not be wanting ye, I'm thinking. Go to the chest and take your share of the linen. Who knows but some man, losing his wife, will be glad to take ye for his second. I'd not have ye going empty-handed to him."

Oona held fast to the dream; she let neither years nor heartaches shatter it. There was always a cabin waiting to welcome her as soon as another had finished with her. From the time when Oona left the Hegarty cabin, a bonny lass still, with strength to her body and laughter in her eyes, to the time when she was put out of the MacManuses', old and with little work left in her, the tale runs thin as gossamer. But if you are knowing Ireland and the people of Donegal, it is not hard to follow the tinker's child through that running of years.

rom cabin to cabin, wherever trouble or need abided, there went Oona. In a cabin where the mother was young, ailing, with her first-born, there you would find Oona caring for the child as it had been her own. In a cabin where the childher had grown and gone dandering off to Belfast, Dublin, or America and left the old ones behind, there she tended them as she would have tended her own had she ever known them. In a cabin where a man had lost his wife and was ill-fitted to mind the house and the weans alone—aye, here she was the happiest. She would be after taking over the brood as a mother would, gentling the hurt that death had left behind, and for herself building afresh the dream.

But her birth betrayed her at every turn of the road. No man trusted her to be his first or second wife. Not one of the many she served and loved guessed of the hunger that grew with the years for a cabin she could call hers. All blessed her name while she lived; and for the hundred years since she has been gone from Carn-na-ween the tales about her have been kept green with loving memory. Those she served saw that she never went empty-handed away. So to Bridget Hegarty's linen was added a griddle, pans, kettles, crocks, creels, and dishes.

Each thing she chose from the cabin she was leaving was something needed to make the home she dreamed of gay and hold comfort. As the years went by, the bundle of her possessions grew, even as she dwindled. Men, women, and childher who passed her on the road at such times as she might be changing cabins would stop to blather with her. Pointing to the size of her bundle, they would say: " 'Tis twice your size, the now. Ye'll have to be asking for oxen

and a cart to fetch it away from the next cabin." And they would laugh. Or they would say: "Ye might be asking the marquis to build ye a castle next his own. Ye'll be needing a fair-sized place to keep all ye've been gathering these many years."

lways she would blather back at them. For all her dream was dimming, she was never one to get down-daunted. "Ye can never be telling," she would say, "I may yet be having a wee cabin of my own someday. I'm not saying how and I'm not saying when." And she would nod her head in a wise, knowledgeable way, as if she could look down the nose of the future and see what was there.

She was in the cabin of the MacManuses when the great famine came. The corn in the fields blighted; the potatoes rotted in the ground. There was neither food for man nor fodder for beast. Babies starved at their mother's breasts, strong men grew weak as childher, dragging themselves into the fields to gnaw at the blistered grass and die under a cruel, drouthing sun. Everywhere could be heard the crying of childher and the keening for the dead. At the beginning, neighbor shared with neighbor until death stalked them. Then it was every cabin for itself, and many a man sat all night, fowling piece across his knee, to keep guard over a last cow in the byre or the last measure of meal in the bin.

So old had Oona grown by famine time that the neighbors had lost all count of her years. She moved slowly on unsteady feet. Her eyes were dulled; her speech was seldom coming now. But for all that, she was worth the sheltering and the scanty food she ate. She milked; she churned; she helped the oldest lad carry the creel to the bog; she helped at the cutting of the turf. So long as there was food enough for them, the MacManuses kept her and blessed the Virgin for another pair of hands to work.

But famine can put stones in the place of human hearts, and hunger can make tongues bitter. As the winter drew in, Oona for all her dullness saw the childher watching every morsel of food she put to her lips. She heard the

mother's tongue sharpen as she counted out the spoonfuls of stirabout that went into the bowls. Harvest had come and gone, and there was no harvest. The cold, cruel winds of December rattled at their doors and windows. Of one thing only was there enough: there was always turf in the bog to cut, to dry, to keep the hearth warm.

The childher in the cabin cried from cockcrow till candle time. Oona wished her ears had been as dulled as her eyes. But for all that, she closed her heart to the crying, telling herself she had earned what little food she took and the good heat for her old body. But a night came when she could stand the crying no longer, when the spoon scraped the bottom of the meal bin, when the last of the prateys had been eaten, their skins with them.

Saying never a word, she got up at last from the creepie, where she had been thawing her bones, and started to put together again her things into her bundle. The MacManuses watched her, and never a word said they. The corners of the great cloth were tied at last. Over her bent shoulders Oona laid her shawl. The cabin was quiet the now, the childher having cried themselves asleep with hunger. Oona dragged her bundle to the door; as she lifted the latch she spoke: "Ye can fend for yourselves. Ye'll not want me the now."

"Aye, 'tis God's truth." It was the wife who said it.

Timothy MacManus reached for her hand. "Hush, are ye not remembering what night it is?"

"Aye, 'tis Christmas Eve. What matter?

There be's not sense enough left in the old one's mind to know it. And in times such as these there is naught to put one night ahead of another."

" 'Twill be a curse on us, the same, if we let her go."

" 'Twill be a curse on her if she stays."

"God and Mary stay with ye this night," Oona called, going out the door.

"God and Mary go with ye," the two mumbled back to her.

utside Oona lifted the bundle to her back. How she had strength for this I cannot be telling you. It often comes, a strange and great strength, to those who have borne much and have need to bear more. Oona took the road leading to Killybegs and the sea. A light snow was falling and the wind had dropped to a low whispering. As she went down the village street she stopped to glimpse each cabin and the lighted room within. Hardly a cabin but she had lived in; hardly a face but she had read long and deeply over many years. Her lips made a blessing and a farewell for every door she passed.

All cabins were left behind as the road grew steeper. She climbed with a prayer on her lips— what prayer I do not know, but it lightened the load she carried on her back and in her heart, it smoothed the roughness of her going. She came at last to the bogland. It stretched on and on beyond the reach of eye, even in the daylight. In the dark she sensed only a leveling off, where feet could rest. She stumbled from the road and found shelter under a blackthorn which grew on the fringe of the bog.

"I like it here," she said as she eased the bundle from her back. "Always, I have liked it here. Many's the time I have said: Some day I will take the whole of it and climb the hill and sit under this very thorn, the way I'll be feeling the wind from the sea and watching the sun set on it, and the stars lighting it; and, mayhap, hearing the sound of fairy pipes. I never came; I never had the day whole."

She said it in a kind of wonder. She was safe here from the reach of neighbors. It was in her heart that she could never again bear to have

man or woman offer her food needed for young mouths. Too many times she had folded tired hands; too many times she had shut weary eyes, not to know what a gentle companioning death could give the old at the end. " 'Tis a friend, he is, that I have known long. 'Tis as a friend he will be coming, calling softly, wishfully, 'Come, Oona!' "

After that her head grew light. She lost all count of time; she lost all track of space. She felt no cold, no tiredness. She could gather years into her mind as cards into the hand, shuffle them about and draw out the ones she liked best. She remembered suddenly that one of the reasons for wanting to climb the hill was to find the fairy rath that lay somewhere along the bog. Conall of a Thousand Songs had slept a Midsummer Night with his head to this rath and had wakened in the morning with it filled full of fairy music—music of enchantment. Wully Donoghue had crossed the rath late one May eve and caught the fairy host riding abroad. Many a time, herself, she had put a piggin of milk with a bowl of stirabout on the back steps of those cabins she had lived in, remembering how well the Gentle People liked milk and stirabout. Aye, the Gentle People, the Good People! She hoped famine had not touched them. It would be a sorry thing to have the fairy folk starved off the earth.

he slept a little, woke, and slept again. Above the sleeping her mind moved on a slow current. Snow had covered her, warm. This was Christmas Eve, the time of the year when no one should go hungry, no one cold. It would be a white Christmas on the morrow, and the people of Donegal had a saying that when a white Christmas came the Gentle People left their raths and trooped abroad to see the wonder of it. Aye, that was a good saying. They would make good company for a lonely old woman.

Her legs were cramping under her. She strove to move them, and as she did so, she had a strange feeling that she had knocked something over. Her old eyes peered into the darkness, her hand groped for whatever it was she had upset. To her amazement, when she held her hand under her eyes there was a fairy man, not a hand high. His wee face was puckered with worry. "Don't ye be afeard, wee man," she clucked to him. "I didn't know ye were after being where ye were. Was there anything at all ye were wanting?"

"Aye, we were wanting ye."

"Me!"

"None else. Look!"

And then she saw the ground about her covered with hundreds upon hundreds of Gentle People, their faces no bigger round than buttons, all raised to hers, all laughing.

"What might ye be laughing at?" she asked. "Tell me, for it be's a lee long time since I had laughter on my own lips."

"We are laughing at ye, tinker's child. Living a lifetime in other folks' cabins, serving and nursing and mothering and loving, and never a cabin or kin ye could call your own."

"Aye," she sighed, "aye, 'tis the truth."

" 'Tis no longer the truth. Bide where ye be, Oona Hegarty, and sleep the while."

She did as she was bidden, but sleep was as thin as the snow which covered her, breaking through in this place and that, so that she might see through it what was going on about her. Hither and yon the Good People were hurrying. They brought stones; they brought turf. They laid a roof tree and thatched it. They built a chimney and put in windows. They hung a door at the front and a door at the back. As they worked they sang, and the song they made drifted into Oona's sleep and stayed with her;

" 'Tis a snug Christmas cabin we're build-
　　ing the night,
　　That we're building the night.
The stones make the walls and the turf
　　chinks it tight,
　　Aye, the turf chinks it tight.
There'll be thatch for the roof to keep
　　wind out and rain,
　　To keep wind out and rain.
And a fire on the hearth to burn out all
　　pain,
　　Aye, burn out all pain.
The meal in the chest will stand up to
　　your chin,
　　Well up to your chin;
There'll be Christmas without, and
　　Christmas within,
　　Always Christmas within.
There'll be plenty of currants, and sugar,
　　and tea,
　　Aye, plenty of tea;
With the chintz at the windows as gay as
　　can be,
　　All as gay as can be."

here was more to the song. It went
on and on, and Oona could not tell
where the song ended and the dream began, so
closely woven were the two together. She felt of
a sudden a small, tweaking hand on her skirt
and heard a shrill voice piping, "Wake up—
wake up, Oona Hegarty!"

" 'Tis awake I am, entirely," said Oona, sit-
ting up and rubbing her eyes. "Awake and
dreaming at the same time, just."

"We'll be after fetching in your bundle, then;
and all things shall find their rightful places at
last."

Ten hundred fairy men lifted the bundle and
bore it inside, with Oona following. She drew
her breath through puckered lips; she let it out
again in sighs of wonderment. "Is everything to
your liking, ma'am?" inquired the fairy man she
had knocked over.

She made the answer as she looked about her:
"The bed's where it should be. The chintz
now—I had a mind to have it green, with a
touch of the sun and a touch of the flaming
turf in it. The dresser is convenient high. Wait

till I have my bundle undone and the treasures
of a lifetime put away."

The Gentle People scuttled about helping
her, putting the linen in the fine oak chest, the
dishes on the dresser. The kettle was hung
above the hearth, the creepie put beside it. The
rug spread along the bedside and the griddle
left standing by the fire, ready. All things in
their right places, as the tinker's child had
dreamed them.

"Is it all to your liking?" shouted the Gentle
People together.

"Aye, 'tis that and more. Crocks and creels
where they do belong. The fine, strong spoon
to be hanging there, ready to stir the griddle
bread. The knife with the sharp edge to it, to be
cutting it." She turned and looked down at the
floor, at the hundreds of wee men crowding her
feet. "I'm not asking why ye have done this
thing for me this night. But I ask one thing
more. On every white Christmas let you be
bringing folk to my door—old ones not needed
longer by others, children crying for their
mother, a lad or a lass for whom life has gone
amiss. Fetch them, that I may warm them by
the hearth and comfort them."

"We will do that, tinker's child; we will do
that!" The voices of the Gentle People drifted
away from her like a wind dying over the bog:
it was there—it was gone. A great sleep took
Oona Hegarty, so that her eyes could stay open
no longer. She put herself down on the outshot
bed. She pulled the warm blanket over her and
drew the chintz curtains.

he next night—Christmas—hunger
drove Maggie, the middle child of
the MacManuses, out of their cabin. She went
like a wee, wild thing, knowing only the hunger pain she bore and the need of staying it.
Blindly she climbed the hill to the bogland.
Weak and stumbling she was, whimpering like
a poor, hurt creature. She stumbled off the road;
she stumbled over the sudden rise on the bog,
which nearly laid her flat. Rubbing her eyes, she
looked up at a wee cabin standing where no
cabin had ever been. Through the windows
came a welcoming light. In wonderment she
lifted the latch and went in.

"Come in, Maggie. I've been looking for ye, the lee long day." It was Oona's voice that spoke to her; aye, but what a changed Oona! She knelt by the hearth turning the griddle bread, her eyes as blue as fairy thimbles, her hair the color of ripened corn. There were prateys boiling in the kettle, tea making on the hearth. Enough to eat and to spare. But that was not what filled the child's eyes with wonder. It was Oona herself, grown young, with the look of a young bride on her. "Take the creepie." Her voice had the low, soft calling of a throstle to its young. "Ye'll be after eating your fill, Maggie, and not knowing hunger again for many a day."

And it's the truth I am telling. Maggie went back and told; but although half of Carn-na-ween hunted the cabin throughout the year, none found it. Not until a white Christmas again came round. Then old Seumus MacIntyre the cobbler died, leaving his widow Molly poor and none to keep her. They were coming to fetch her to the workhouse that Christmas Eve when she took the road climbing to Killybegs and the sea, and was never seen again.

And so the tales run. There are enough to be filling a book, but why should I go on with them? You can be after telling them to yourselves. This I know: given a white Christmas this year, the wee fairy cabin of Carn-na-ween will be having its latch lifted through the night by the lone and the lost and the heartbroken. Aye, Oona Hegarty, the tinker's child, will be keeping the griddle hot, the kettle full, and her arms wide to the childher of half the world this night—if it be's a white Christmas.

Irish crafts

Turnip Candleholder*

In Ireland, it is a Christmas tradition to place lighted candles in the front windows of the house. In the past, many families did not own enough candleholders, so they improvised. Turnips were plentiful and both large and heavy enough to hold a candle. What the Irish refer to as a turnip is called a rutabaga in America.

Materials

- rutabaga
- paring knife
- candle (preferably a drip candle)
- small plate or plastic lid
- holly and greens

1. Cut off the top and bottom of the turnip (rutabaga) with the paring knife. The bottom should be trimmed flat.

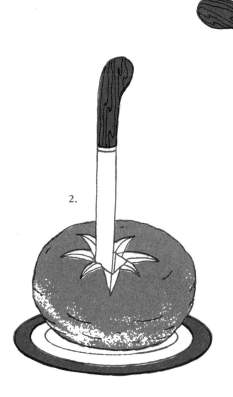

2. Core a hole in the turnip big enough to hold the candle. (Use an apple corer, if one is available.) Using the paring knife, cut notches around the core hole to create a star pattern (see illustration to left).

3. Place the candle in the turnip. A red or green candle that will drip wax down over the surface of the turnip will produce the most pleasing effect. If the core hole is slightly larger than the candle, pour a little hot wax into the hole; while the wax is still soft, insert the candle into the hole, making sure it is standing up straight. Place the turnip candleholder on a small plate or plastic lid that is larger than the base of the turnip. Decorate around the bottom of the turnip with holly and greens.

---

* This craft should not be attempted without adult supervision.

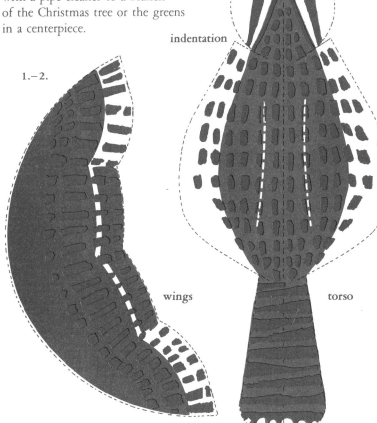

St. Stephen's Day Wren

In Ireland, the wren is considered the "king of all birds." While not mighty, the little wren is, nevertheless, ultimately triumphant because it is clever. The Irish may think of the wren as a symbol of themselves. The bird is particularly important during the Christmas season. On December 26, St. Stephen's Day, the children of the country "go on the wren," that is, they carry a symbolic wren door-to-door, chanting rhymes and begging treats. It is one of the most festive, fun-filled days of the year.

Materials

- paper (both tracing paper or onion-skin *and* heavy, white construction paper)
- needle and thread, or pipe cleaner
- crayons or dry markers or tempera paint (orange, brown, and white)
- scissors (If children are involved, use snub-nosed scissors.)

The St. Stephen's Day wren can be hung with thread or anchored with a pipe cleaner to a branch of the Christmas tree or the greens in a centerpiece.

1.–2.

indentation

wings

torso

1. The wren can be made by cutting out the wings and body patterns on this page or by tracing the patterns and coloring your own bird. If you trace the bird, include the eyes and markings. Turn the tracing paper over and rub the outline and markings with the broad side of a lead pencil. Place the tracing paper, pencil rubbings down, on a sheet of construction paper and retrace the outline and markings; this will transfer the outline, etc., from the tracing paper to the construction paper. Using a crayon or dry marker, reoutline the torso and wings on the construction paper. Next, color in your bird with either crayon, dry marker, or tempera paint. Note how the dots and strokes on the pattern give the impression of feathers. Also, see the wren article in Volume 21 of *The World Book Encyclopedia* for a color illustration of the winter wren.

2. Cut out the torso and wings. The slight indentations between the head and the body must be cut as well. Cut slots along the dotted lines on the wren's body.

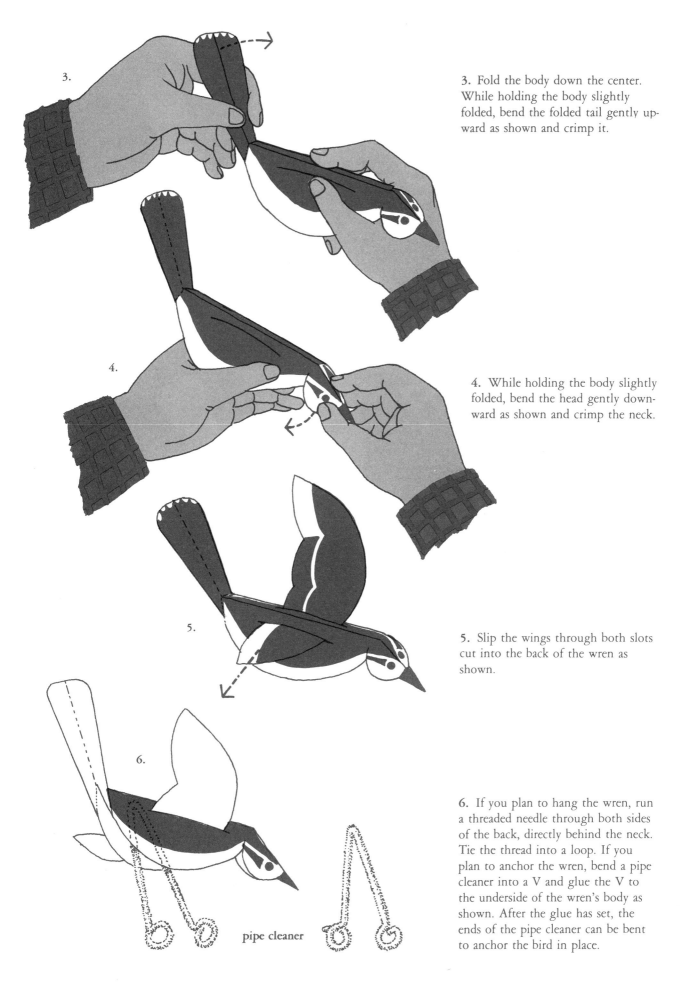

3. Fold the body down the center. While holding the body slightly folded, bend the folded tail gently upward as shown and crimp it.

4. While holding the body slightly folded, bend the head gently downward as shown and crimp the neck.

5. Slip the wings through both slots cut into the back of the wren as shown.

6. If you plan to hang the wren, run a threaded needle through both sides of the back, directly behind the neck. Tie the thread into a loop. If you plan to anchor the wren, bend a pipe cleaner into a V and glue the V to the underside of the wren's body as shown. After the glue has set, the ends of the pipe cleaner can be bent to anchor the bird in place.

pipe cleaner

Thatched Cottages*

The Irish countryside is still dotted with the traditional housing of Ireland—cottages. Built of stone that is whitewashed inside and out, the cottages feature thatched roofs woven from straw. If properly cared for, the roofs can last for over a century and are, in Ireland, considered something of an art form. Extraordinary patterns are often interwoven in the straw thatch. Each pattern is unique and identifies an individual craftsman, whose style may be based upon Celtic symbols or family tradition. In an effort to keep the craft alive, competitions that judge speed, skill, and style are held throughout the country.

Materials

- matchboxes (either small or large, kitchen-type)
- glue (white, all-purpose)
- paper (heavy, stiff paper stock)
- fabric (scraps of wool, linen, or homespun in both light and dark colors)
- scissors (If children are involved, use snub-nosed scissors.)

1. A miniature thatched cottage can be made in a variety of sizes: small, kitchen matchbox size, or double. If you choose to make a double-sized cottage, pull the matchbox drawer out of the sleeve. Glue two drawers together, end-to-end, as shown. After the glue has set, slip the sleeves back over the joined drawers.

2. Use a piece of white or light-colored fabric for the walls of the cottage. Cut the fabric to cover three sides of the matchbox, as shown. Using this rectangle of fabric as a pattern, cut a piece of darker fabric (either a solid, stripe, or tweed) to the same size. Also cut a piece of heavy, stiff paper to the same size. Put the paper and darker fabric aside to use for the roof. Glue the light-colored fabric to the three sides of your matchbox.

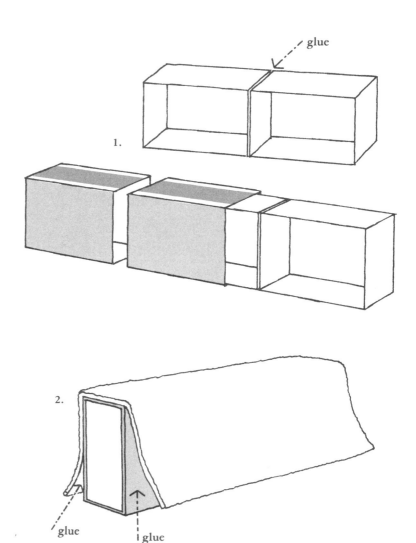

3. Glue the darker fabric to the paper. After the glue has set, crease the assembly to form a U or V (see below).

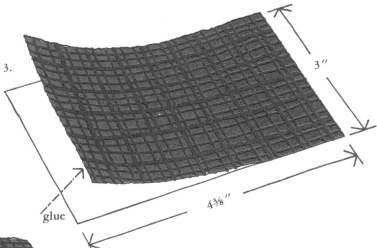

3.

3"

4⅜"

glue

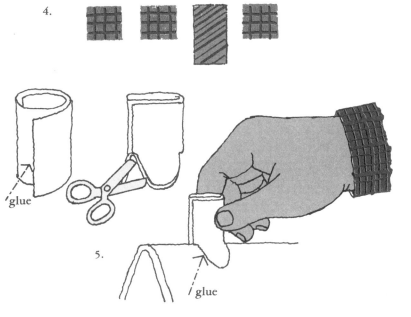

4. Place the roof over the matchbox cottage, as shown. The roof should extend down over the walls on both sides. This will form eaves, as well as allow space for glue. Glue the roof to the walls of the cottage. Cut doors and windows out of a fabric darker than the walls of the house. (If possible, use a tiny plaid, windowpane check, or tweed for the windows.) Glue the doors and windows to the sides of the house.

4.

glue

5.

glue

glue

5. Using the same light-colored fabric used for the walls, cut a one-inch square for each chimney. (A double-sized cottage looks better with two chimneys. If you are using a kitchen-sized matchbox, enlarge the square to two and one-half inches.) Spread glue on one end of the square and roll the opposite end into the glued end. The fabric should be overlapped three or four times. Squeeze the roll so that the glue spreads evenly. After the glue has set, cut two slots, one opposite the other, at one end of this cylinder, as shown. Dab a bit of glue on the flaps created by the slots and push the flaps down over the ridge of the roof.

An entire village can be assembled in this way. (Irish villages often consist of no more than seven or eight houses.) A village church can be constructed by gluing four kitchen-type matchboxes into a block. Add a high roof in the same manner described above. Cut longer windows and doors that terminate in a pointed arch. A flat or even a saw-toothed steeple can be added by turning a matchbox on end and attaching it to the front of the other four boxes.

---

* Completed examples of the thatched cottage craft are illustrated on the *Christmas in Ireland* recipe cards.

Irish recipes

Irish Christmas Pudding

½ cup currants
½ cup Sultana raisins, chopped
½ citron, chopped
½ cup preserved cherries, chopped
2 cups Irish whiskey
¾ cup flour
2 cups breadcrumbs
1 cup brown sugar
¼ cup suet, finely chopped
½ tsp. salt
½ tsp. nutmeg
½ tsp. allspice
¼ tsp. ginger
1 cup almonds, chopped
1 apple, peeled and grated
grated rind and juice of 2 lemons
4 eggs
1 cup stout (or apple juice)
1 tbsp. butter

(1) Combine the fruit ingredients in a large nonmetal bowl. Add 1 cup of Irish whiskey, cover, and allow to stand for 12 hours. (2) Mix together the flour, breadcrumbs, sugar, suet, salt, and spices. (3) Blend in the almonds, grated apples, whiskey-soaked fruit, and lemon rind and juice. (4) Beat the eggs to a froth. (5) Add the stout (or apple juice) to the eggs and combine this with the flour mixture. Work the eggs/stout in a little at a time, blending well. (6) Grease two 6-inch bowls with butter and pour the pudding into the bowls, filling them two-thirds full. (7) Cover the bowls with either floured muslin or a double layer of wax paper tied into place. (8) Place the bowls in a large kettle and pour in sufficient water to come three quarters of the way up the bowls. (9) Bring this to a boil, then lower the heat and simmer for 5½ to 6 hours, adding more water as needed. (10) Remove the cloth or wax paper covering. (11) Allow the puddings to cool before removing them from the bowls. (12) Place the puddings on plates and pour remaining Irish whiskey over the puddings. Allow them to stand until they soak up the whiskey. (13) Wrap the puddings in cheesecloth, place them in airtight containers, and store them in the refrigerator for at least 2 to 3 weeks. (14) To serve the puddings, put them back into their bowls. Place the bowls in simmering water and heat for 2 to 3 hours. (15) Flame with Irish whiskey or brandy just before serving.

Christmas Cookies

1 cup butter, room temperature
1 cup sugar
3 eggs
2 cups flour
¼ cup Irish whiskey
¼ cup candied citron, chopped
¼ cup golden raisins, blanched and chopped
¼ cup almonds, chopped

(1) Preheat oven to 375°. (2) Cream butter and sugar. (3) Beat in eggs until well blended. (4) Add flour and Irish whiskey and beat until smooth. (5) Add fruit and nuts and mix well. (6) Drop dough from a tablespoon onto greased cookie sheet and bake for 8 to 10 minutes. (7) Remove from sheet with spatula while the cookies are still warm.

Mince Tartlets

Mincemeat
1 large apple
2 cups dark seedless raisins
1 cup golden raisins
2 cups currants
½ cup candied fruit peel
½ cup almonds
1 orange
1 lemon
1 cup sugar
¼ tsp. salt
¼ tsp. cinnamon
¼ tsp. allspice
¼ tsp. powdered cloves
½ cup melted butter
¼ cup Irish whiskey

(1) Core, but do not peel, the apple. (2) Mince the apple, raisins, currants, fruit peel, and almonds at the coarse setting of the mincer. (3) Grate the rind from the lemon and orange and squeeze out the juice. (4) Mix the grated rind with the sugar, salt, and spices. (5) Add the melted butter and spiced sugar to the minced fruit. (6) Add the lemon juice, orange juice, and whiskey to the minced fruit. (7) Mix thoroughly with the hand. (8) Store in airtight jars until needed.

Pie Crust
¾ cup butter (cold)
2¼ cups all-purpose flour
salt
ice water

(1) Rub the butter into the salted flour. (2) Bind to a stiff dough with a little ice water. (3) Chill for 1 hour. (4) Roll out the pastry very thinly. (5) Cut into 3½-inch rounds with a pastry cutter. (6) Ease half of the rounds onto a greased 2½-inch tart pan. (7) Drop 2 to 3 tablespoons of mincemeat into the center of each round and cover with another round of pastry. (8) Pinch the sides together so that the "top hat" will not come off in the cooking. (9) With the point of a knife, make a cut into the top of each tartlet to allow steam to escape. (10) Bake at 400° for approximately 15 to 20 minutes; the pastry should be golden in color. (11) Serve the tartlets hot with a dusting of confectioners' sugar.

Almond Paste or Marzipan*

(Icing for Christmas Cake)

5 cups ground almonds
3½ cups sifted confectioners' sugar
1 cup sugar
4 eggs
juice of 1 lemon
1 tsp. vanilla
1 tbsp. rum
1 tbsp. orange-flower water

(1) Crush confectioners' sugar with a rolling pin and sieve well. (2) Mix the confectioners' sugar, granulated sugar, and almonds. (3) Beat the eggs, gradually adding the lemon juice, vanilla, rum, and orange-flower water. (4) First with a wooden spoon and then with the hand, mix the egg mixture with the dry ingredients until there is a paste. NOTE: While it is essential to work the marzipan into a smooth paste, it must not be overhandled or it will become crumbly, brittle, and difficult to roll and mold. (5) After kneading the paste, wrap it in wax paper, cover it, and leave for 24 hours when it will be easier to handle. (6) Roll the marzipan, on a board lightly coated with confectioners' sugar, into a 14-inch circle. (7) Drape the circle of marzipan over the cake, triming the bottom as necessary. (8) Wrap the cake in foil and store it in a dry, cool place for several days.

* Commercial almond paste (marzipan) is available and can be used to ice the Christmas cake. Use 3 (7 oz.) tubes. Follow instructions 6, 7, and 8 above.

Royal Frosting

(Frosting for Christmas Cake)

Original recipe

4 egg whites
7 cups sifted confectioners' sugar
¼ tsp. acetic acid
3 drops laundry bluing

(1) Place the carefully separated egg whites in a bowl that has been scalded and allowed to dry. (2) Slightly beat the egg whites for a minute or long enough to make them liquid. (3) Crush and sieve the confectioners' sugar. (4) Add half the sugar to the egg whites and beat lightly for about 2 minutes. NOTE: Do no skimp on the beating; royal frosting must be beaten until it becomes smooth and stiff. (5) Add the remainder of the sugar gradually, beating well after each addition. NOTE: Do not use more than the minimum of sugar necessary to get the frosting to the required consistency. (6) Before the frosting is quite stiff enough, add ¼ teaspoon of acetic acid. (Do not use lemon juice.) (7) At the last minute—to make sure that the frosting will be "as white and pure as the driven snow"—beat in 3 drops of ordinary laundry bluing. Do not worry if the frosting looks a little blue. This will disappear in beating. The frosting will dry out quite white. Do not use more than 3 drops of weak bluing, or the frosting will have a grayish tinge. (8) Using a spatula occasionally dipped in hot water, spread the frosting over the top and sides of the cake. (9) After the frosting is quite dry, decorate the cake with a stiffer version of the royal frosting. Decide upon a design. Prick it out with a darning needle. For good effect, do your writing or trellist work with a No. 2 pastry tube in white frosting; when this is dry, go over it with pink frosting, using a No. 1 tube.

Modern recipe

4 egg whites
6 cups of confectioners' sugar
⅛ tsp. cream of tartar

(1) Beat the egg whites and cream of tartar until they are frothy. (2) Slowly add the confectioners' sugar. (3) Beat until the frosting is stiff. (4) Using a spatula, spread the frosting over the top and sides of the cake. (5) Decorate with holly leaves.

Soda Scones

3 cups flour
1 tsp. cream of tartar
1 cup buttermilk
1 tsp. salt
1 tsp. baking soda

(1) Stir together the flour, cream of tartar, salt, and baking soda and mix lightly with the hands. (2) Make a hollow in the center and add enough buttermilk to make a soft dough. (3) Turn onto a floured board and knead quickly and lightly until the dough is free from cracks. (4) Roll out into a circle about ½-inch thick. (5) Cut into wedges (as if cutting a pie). (6) Place on a greased and floured baking sheet and bake at 400° for approximatley 15 minutes.

Spiced Beef

Spicing ingredients
3 bay leaves
1 tsp. cloves (whole)
¼ tsp. mace
1 level tsp. peppercorns
1 clove garlic
1 tsp. allspice (whole)
2 heaping Tbsp. brown sugar
2 heaping tsp. saltpetre (optional)
½ cup coarse rock salt

Cooking ingredients
brisket of beef (6 lbs)
1 celery stick
1 medium-sized onion
3 cloves (whole)
3 carrots (sliced)
1 tsp. cloves (ground)
1 tsp. allspice
½ pint stout

(1) Mix dry ingredients together, pounding in bay leaves and garlic. (2) Stand the brisket of beef in a large dish and rub the spicing mixture over the meat. (3) Leave the beef in the spicing mixture for one week (refrigerated). (4) Turn the brisket daily, rubbing the meat in the spicing mixture from the bottom of the dish. (5) At the end of the week, wash the meat and tie it for cooking. (6) Place the brisket in a pot on a bed of chopped vegetables and spices. (7) Add enough water to cover the brisket. (8) Bring the water to a boil. (9) Skim the top of the water. (10) Simmer the brisket for 4 to 5 hours, adding the stout during the last hour.

Dressed Whole Salmon

Ingredients
whole salmon (4 to 6 pounds)
salt and pepper
bay leaves
lemon slices
onion slices

Garnish
lemon
parsley
lettuce leaves
tomatoes
cucumber

(1) Clean and gut the salmon. (2) Wrap it in a piece of cheesecloth to help in removing the fish from the saucepan. This is not necessary if you have a fish poacher. (3) Add salt, pepper, bay leaves, onion slices, and lemon slices to boiling water. (4) Lower the salmon into the boiling water and bring back to a boil. (5) Then gently simmer 5 minutes per pound of salmon. (6) After the cooking is completed, leave the salmon in the water for 5 minutes. (7) Lift the fish out and drain. (8) Remove the skin. (9) Decorate the salmon with savory butter and garnish with lettuce leaves, lemon, parsley, tomatoes, and cucumber.

Carrageen Moss Jelly

¼ ounce Carrageen*
1 pint milk
lemon rind
1 tbsp. sugar
pinch of salt

(1) Wash the moss and steep for 10 to 15 minutes. (2) Place the moss into a saucepan with milk, salt, and lemon rind. (3) Bring this to a boil and simmer until it coats the back of a wooden spoon. (4) Stir in the sugar. (5) Strain into a wet mold and leave in a cool place to set.

* Carrageen (*Chondrus crispus*) is an edible seaweed frequently used in Ireland. It is gathered particularly around the west coast in April and May, washed, and left to bleach in the sun.

Broiled Irish Ham

1 ham (12 lbs.)
1 quart Irish stout
½ cup sugar
2 tbsp. breadcrumbs
2 tbsp. brown sugar
cloves

(1) Soak the ham in cold water for 24 hours. (2) Place the ham in a large pot with the stout, granulated sugar, and enough water to cover the meat. (3) Very slowly, bring the pot to a boil and then simmer for 20 to 25 minutes per pound. NOTE: If the ham is cooked too fast, it will become tough and stringy. (4) After the cooking is completed, allow the ham to sit in the liquid for at least one half-hour.* (5) Remove the ham from the pot and peel the skin. (6) Cover the surface of the ham with a mixture of breadcrumbs and brown sugar. (7) Stud the ham generously with cloves. (8) Place the ham on a broiling pan or baking dish and return it to a hot oven for color.

* For cold ham, allow the joint to cool completely in the liquid and do not color in the oven.

Apple and Bread Dressing

(Alternate stuffing for Christmas goose)

1 lb. wheat bread, cubed and dried (fresh, not croutons)
1 cup butter
2 cups finely chopped onions
2 cups finely chopped celery
1 cup stock (can be made from neck, gizzards, liver)
½ cup chopped fresh parsley
1 tsp. salt
½ tsp. pepper
2 eggs, beaten
¼ cup raisins
2 cups finely diced apples (Jonathan or Winesap)
¼ cup chopped pecans (optional ingredient)

(1) Sauté the onions and celery in the cup of butter. (2) Mix this with the other ingredients, including the seasonings. (3) Stuff the goose and secure the flap with a skewer. Do not stuff the goose too full as the dressing swells during the roasting.

Irish Soda Bread

White bread
1 lb. all-purpose flour
1 cup sour milk
½ tsp. baking soda
½ tsp. salt

Brown bread
10 ounces whole-wheat flour
6 ounces all-purpose flour
1 cup sour milk
½ tsp. baking soda
½ tsp. salt

(1) Sieve the dry ingredients together and make a well in the center.

NOTE: If making brown bread, do not sieve the whole-wheat flour; sieve other dry ingredients and simply add the flour. (2) Add enough milk to make a thick dough. Mix this well with a wooden spoon, bringing the flour into the center from the sides. Add more milk if the mixture seems too stiff. (3) Lift the mixture onto a floured board and knead lightly. (4) Flatten the dough into a circle. (5) Place the dough onto a baking sheet. With a floured knife, score the top in the form of a cross. (6) Bake at 400° for about 40 minutes.

Irish carols

WEXFORD CAROL (CHRISTMAS)

English and Irish traditional

Irish traditional (M.S.)

1. Good peo-ple all,— this Christ-mas-time, Con-si-der well— and
2. The night be-fore— that hap-py tide, The no-ble Vir- gin

bear in mind What our good— God— for us has done, In
and her guide Were long time— seek - ing up and down To

send-ing his— be-lo-ved Son. With Ma-ry ho— ly
find a lodg - ing in the town. But mark how all— things

we should pray To— God with love— this Christ-mas Day; In
came to pass: From e - v'ry door— re - pell'd, a - las! As

Beth - le - hem— up-on that morn There was a bless-ed Mes-si - ah born.
long fore-told,— their re-fuge all Was but an hum - ble ox-'s stall.

From the *Oxford Book of Carols*. By permission of Oxford University Press.

IRISH CAROL (CHRISTMAS)

Irish traditional

Ibid.
(M.S.)

1. Christ-mas Day is come; let's all pre-pare for mirth, Which fills the heav'ns and earth at this a-maz-ing birth. Through both the joy-ous an-gels in strife and hur-ry fly, With glo-ry and ho-san-nas, 'All Ho-ly' do they cry, In heav'n the Church tri-um-phant a-dores with all her choirs, The

2. But why should we re-joice? Should we not ra-ther mourn To see the hope of na-tions thus in a sta-ble born? Where are his crown and scep-tre, where is his throne sub-lime, Where is his train ma-jes-tic that should the stars out-shine? Is there no sump-tuous pa-lace nor a-ny inn at all To

(Bass) *Ding dong, ding dong, etc.*

Sop. (In (Is

A.+T. *Ding* dong, ding dong, ding dong, ding dong, ding dong, ding dong, ding

mi - li-tant on earth__ with hum - ble faith ad - mires. In
lodge his heav'n-ly mo - ther__ but in a fil - thy stall? Is

1st time

dong, ding dong, ding dong, with hum - ble__ faith__ ad - mires. Ding
but in a __ fil - thy__ stall?

(Bass) Ding dong, ding dong, ding dong, ding

hum - ble faith ad - mires._____
in a fil - thy stall?_____

2nd time

hum - ble__ faith__ ad - mires, with__ hum - ble__ faith__ ad - mires.
in a __ fil - thy__ stall, but__ in __ a __ fil - thy__ stall?

dong, ding dong, ding dong, ding dong, ding dong, ding dong.

3 Oh! cease, ye blessèd angels, such clamorous joys
    to make!
   Though midnight silence favours, the shepherds are
    awake;
   And you, O glorious star! that with new splendour
    brings
   From the remotest parts three learnèd eastern kings,
   Turn somewhere else your lustre, your rays elsewhere
    display;
   For Herod he may slay the babe, and Christ must
    straight away.

4 If we would then rejoice, let's cancel the old score,
   And, purposing amendment, resolve to sin no more—
   For mirth can ne'er content us, without a conscience
    clear;
   And thus we'll find true pleasure in all the usual cheer,
   In dancing, sporting, revelling, with masquerade and
    drum,
   So let our Christmas merry be, as Christians doth
    become.

From the *Oxford Book of Carols*. By permission of Oxford University Press.

SAINT STEPHEN (DEC. 26 AND OTHER OCCASIONS)

Traditional

Ibid.
(M.S.)

1. Saint Ste-phen was a ho-ly man, En-dued with heav'n-ly might, And many won-ders he did work Be-fore the peo-ple's sight; And by the bless-ed Spi-rit of God, Which did his heart in-flame,
2. Be-fore the el-ders was he brought His ans-wer for to make; But they could not the spi-rit with-stand, Where-by this man did speak. Whilst this was told, the mul-ti-tude, Be-hold-ing him a-right,

(1.) He spa-red not, in e-v'ry place,
(2.) His come-ly face be-gan to shine

1.) He spa-red not, in e-v'ry place, To
2.) His come-ly face be-gan to shine Most

(1.) He spa-red not, in e-v'ry place,
(2.) His come-ly face be-gan to shine

1.) He spa-red not, in e-v'ry place,
2.) His come-ly face be-gan to shine

CHORUS

preach God's ho-ly name: O man, do ne-ver
like an an-gel bright:

3 Then Stephen did put forth his voice,
  And he did first unfold
The wondrous works which God hath wrought,
  Even for their fathers old;
That they thereby might plainly know
  Christ Jesus should be he,
That from the burden of the law
  Should quit us frank and free:

  O man, etc.

4 'But, O,' quoth he, 'you wicked men!
  Which of the prophets all
Did not your fathers persecute
  And keep in woeful thrall?'
But when they heard him so to say
  Upon him they all ran,
And then without the city gates
  They stoned this holy man:

  O man, etc.

5 There he most meekly on his knees
  To God did pray at large,
Desiring that he would not lay
  This sin unto their charge;
Then yielding up his soul to God,
  Who had it dearly bought,
He lost his life, whose body then
  To grave was seemly brought:

  O man, etc.

Acknowledgments

Cover:	Bob Willoughby	32:	Fionnbar Callanan
2:	Bob Willoughby	33:	Bob Willoughby
6:	City of Manchester Art Galleries	34:	Trinity College, Dublin (Art Resource)
9:	(Top) Slide File	37:	Slide File
	(Bottom) Nicholas Devore III, Bruce Coleman Inc.	38:	Dennis Brack, Black Star
10:	Slide File	39:	(Top) Bob Willoughby
12:	Bord Fáilte		(Bottom) Dennis Brack, Black Star
13:	Fionnbar Callanan	40:	Slide File
14:	Bord Fáilte	43:	Mary Evans Picture Library
15:	Martin Rogers, FPG	44:	Bord Fáilte
16:	Slide File	45:	Bord Fáilte
17:	Bob Willoughby	46:	(Top) Fionnbar Callanan
18:	Bob Willoughby		(Bottom) Bord Fáilte
19:	Bord Fáilte	47:	Fionnbar Callanan
21:	(Top) Irish Tourist Board	48:	Fionnbar Callanan
	(Bottom) Bob Willoughby	49:	Slide File
22:	Bord Fáilte	50:	Slide File
23:	Bord Fáilte	52:	Illustrated London News Picture Library
24:	Bob Willoughby	53:	Fionnbar Callanan
27:	(Top) Mary Rowley	55:	Slide File
	(Bottom) Tom Kennedy, Source	56:	Slide File
28:	Bob Willoughby	59:	Farrell Grehan, Photo Researchers
29:	Irish Tourist Board	61:	Ron Sanford, Black Star
31:	Bord Fáilte	63:	Ron Sanford, Black Star
		64:	Slide File